The Eschatology
of the
Old Testament

The Eschatology of the Old Testament

GEERHARDUS VOS

EDITED BY
James T. Dennison Jr.

P&R PUBLISHING
P.O. BOX 817 • PHILLIPSBURG • NEW JERSEY 08865-0817

Page design by Tobias Design
Typesetting by Michelle Feaster

Printed in the United States of America

Library of Congress Cataloging-in-Publication Data

Vos, Geerhardus, 1862–1949.
    The eschatology of the Old Testament / Geerhardus Vos; edited by James T. Dennison, Jr.
        p. cm.
    Includes bibliographical references and index.
    ISBN-10: 0-87552-181-9
    ISBN-13: 978-0-87552-181-7
    1. Eschatology—Biblical teaching. 2. Bible. O.T.—Criticism, interpretation, etc. I. Dennison, James T., 1943– II. Title.

BS1199.E75 V67 2001
236'.09'01—dc21
                                                            2001021895

CONTENTS

EDITOR'S PREFACE

Vos's "Old Testament Eschatology" manuscript is a composite document. No complete version of his lecture notes or finished manuscript is extant. Although he began to teach the course in 1917, few student notebooks or syllabi survive (unlike the mimeograph copies of his *Biblical Theology: Old and New Testaments*). In 1975, Vos's daughter, Marianne (Mrs. William) Radius, prevailed upon his son, Dr. Johannes G. Vos of Geneva College, to examine the remains of his father's papers and bring them to Toledo, Ohio. Among the papers were the following: (1) outline notes on the "Eschatology of the Old Testament" in Vos's hand; (2) "Syllabus of the Eschatology of the Old Testament," property of Geerhardus Vos, October 13, 1930—lent to the class of 1930–31 for mimeographing (this manuscript is handwritten by Vos); (3) an incomplete typescript entitled "Some Remarks on Eschatology," which was certainly to be a major work on the subject; the pages to the latter run from 1–58, 138, 169, 226, 228, 255, 310, 348, 355, 382; (4) a set of "Questions in Eschatology of the Old Testament" in Vos's hand; (5) a typescript of notes taken by Henry Schultze entitled "Old Testament Eschatology." All these materials are deposited in the Heritage Hall Archive of Calvin College and Seminary, Grand Rapids, Michigan.

I have attempted to weave together these various sources to provide the most complete text possible of Vos's materials on Old Testament eschatology. Throughout, the reader will notice Vos's keen interaction with the critical schools of the nineteenth and early twentieth centuries (i.e., Wellhausen, Gunkel, and Gressmann). Throughout, he remains a firm supernaturalist, committed to the unenlightened notion of revelation in history.

In this edited version, I have checked and corrected (where necessary) all Scripture citations; transliterated Hebrew and Greek phrases; and provided full bibliographic citations for sources cited by Vos. My manuscript was first reduced to typescript by my mother, Mrs. James T. (Elizabeth G.) Dennison, Denver, Colorado. She gave unselfishly of her time at an IBM Seletrix long before the days of word processors. *Gratias tibi ago, mater!*

LIST OF ABBREVIATIONS

ANET James B. Pritchard, ed. *Ancient Near Eastern Texts Relating to the Old Testament*. Princeton, N.J.: Princeton University Press, 1955.

EB English Bible

ERE James Hastings, ed. *Encyclopaedia of Religion and Ethics*. Edinburgh: T. & T. Clark, 1908–26.

FC Fathers of the Church. Washington, D.C.: Catholic University of America Press.

Loeb The Loeb Classical Library. Cambridge, Mass.: Harvard University Press.

PG Jacques Paul Migne. Patrologiae . . . series Graeca. Paris: J.-P. Migne, 1857–87.

PL Jacques Paul Migne. Patrologiae . . . series Latina. Paris: Garnieri Fratres, 1878.

ZAW *Zeitschrift für die Alttestamentliche Wissenschaft.*

1

INTRODUCTION

Definition

Etymologically, the term *eschatology* (*eschatos logos*) means "a doctrine of the last things." Eschatology deals with the expectation of beliefs characteristic of some religions that: (a) the world or part of the world moves to a definite goal (*telos*); (b) there is a new final order of affairs beyond the present. It is the doctrine of the consummation of the world-process in a supreme crisis leading on into a permanent state. As such, it is composed of two characteristic elements: (1) the limited duration of the present order of things; (2) the eternal character of the subsequent state. The correlate of eschatology is creation.

Whether one feels capable of conceiving it or accepting it depends ultimately on his concept of God. A God who cannot create cannot consummate things because he is conditioned by something outside himself that will not lend itself to him for the execution of a set purpose and for the plastic handling of what is antecedently given to him toward that end. For eschatology, God needs not only to be the Potter sovereign with reference to the clay, but he needs to be a Potter who can produce his own clay with reference to its tractableness. Moreover, a God who is unable to do this or is uncertain of accomplishing this does not by nature fit into the role of a producer or guide of a truly eschatological process. He cannot know from the outset whether he will be successful or not. It is at this point that predestinarianism and eschatology are one at their root.

Biblical Data for the Formation of the Name

The term *eschatology* is taken from the Greek Scriptures (the Septuagint). It has the form *eschatai hemerai*, with certain unessential variations. The Hebrew from which this Greek rendering is derived is *acherith hajjamim* (also *acherith hazza'am* and *acherith hashshanim*). The Hebrew has the following twofold sense: (1) the concluding days of the present order; (2) the days of the subsequent order of things. The former is the more prevailing usage. One of the rare instances of the latter is found in Isaiah 2:2 (= Mic. 4:1). In this passage, *acherith* retains its common meaning, i.e., "the tail-end" of something, either in space or in time. Therefore, *acherith hajjamim* means the tail-tip of the days, i.e., of the course of history. Only it is never purely chronological. There enters into it the element of "outcome." The head may be prophetic of the tail; and the end of the tail may be prophetic of the other end, the tail-tip. Thus the *acherith hajjamim* is the stretch of history toward the end; that in which the course of events comes to rest because it has reached its goal.

In the New Testament, varying formulas occur:

a. "the last days"—*eschatai hemerai* (Acts 2:17; 2 Tim. 3:1; James 5:3; 2 Peter 3:3)

b. "the latter part of the days"—*eschaton ton hemeron touton* (Heb. 1:2)

c. "the last day(s)"—*eschate hemera* (John 6:39, 40, 44, 54; 11:24; 12:48)

d. "the last of the times"—*eschaton ton chronon* (1 Peter 1:20)

e. "the last time"—*eschatos chronos* (Jude 18)

2

f. "the last season"—*eschatos kairos* (1 Peter 1:5)
g. "the last hour"—*eschate hora* (1 John 2:18)[1]
h. Compare: "the last Adam"—*ho eschatos Adam* (1 Cor. 15:45); "the last trumpet"—*he eschate salpiggi* (1 Cor. 15:52); "the consummation of the world"—*sunteleia aionos* (Matt. 13:39, 40, 49; 24:3; 28:20; Heb. 9:26)

The Old and New Testament usage in general designates the section of time preceding the final state of blessedness. Save for a couple of probable exceptions, it does not mean the blessed state, or the crisis. It means: (1) the last of time; (2) the last time including eternity.

The Old Testament Usage

a. In Daniel 10:14, it covers the whole historical development, including the time from the beginning of the Persian regime to the time of deliverance.
b. In Deuteronomy 31:29, Moses designates the captivity as the latter days beyond which lies the deliverance.
c. Ezekiel 38:16 refers to the victory over the last enemy, but still remains on this side of the blessed time.
d. In Jeremiah 23:20, the latter days are spoken of as the time in which Israel had reached an understanding of Jehovah's judgments. Although it is probable that this lies before the turning point, this passage is open to doubt.
e. Jeremiah 49:39 predicts the bringing back of Elam from captivity, thus before the great change comes.
f. Deuteronomy 4:30 places the return of Israel after the judgment was placed in the latter days, therefore prior to the change.
g. In Hosea 3:5, the conversion of Israel and its coming unto God's goodness is described. This is only the movement toward the final state.

h. Numbers 24:14 speaks of the conquest of Moab in the latter days by the star out of Jacob (v. 17).

i. Isaiah 2:2 and Micah 4:1 foretell that in the latter days the mountain of Jehovah will be established. This description of the established existence can mean the final state.

j. Genesis 49:10 describes the state introduced by Shiloh. Therefore the meaning here may also be extended. It is not improbable that the Old Testament writers used this as a general technical term.

The New Testament Usage

In the New Testament, *eschatai hemerai* is restricted and never means the future era. Rather, it refers to the closing era of the first world-period (i.e., present development). This is due to the fact that the Old Testament writers described the final era in terms of time, i.e., a series of days. In the New Testament, it is spoken of as an eternity in distinction from time. In other words, the word *days* fit better into the horizontal perspective of the Old Testament, which conceived even the future world in forms of time rather than in the transcendental aspect of the later eschatology which had learned to distinguish between time and eternity. Thus, the New Testament usage does not include the period of consummation itself. The Old Testament translators felt this distinction and translated it as the latter days, as if there were two series of days, the earlier and the latter. This is clearly indicated by the Hebrew word *'achar*.

The English Bible

As regards the English Bible, a distinction ought to be observed between the Old Testament and New Testament in rendering the phrase *eschatai hemerai*. With few exceptions, the

English Bible reads, in the Old Testament, "the latter days," whereas in the New Testament, the translation is regularly "the last days." This difference is not accidental, nor is it by any means unimportant. It reveals the difference in eschatological outlook and perspective. The Old Testament consciousness looked forward in a horizontal line. It did not look or speak as though it were itself in the midst of the great coming turnover of things. The things pertaining to that were relatively remote. They are not "these days," but a different future group or succession of days. Hence the comparative degree, "the latter days." Futurity and a certain time-distance of these days called "hindmost days" is implied. The Old Testament feels a certain number of miles removed from arrival at the goal. "The latter days" is the time-stretch that from a distance can be recognized to be closer to the destination, but cannot be quite surveyed. There remains the effect of the relativity of vision. A certain indeterminateness continues to cleave to the form of representation. It is like measuring a nebulous distance with the rod made for measuring a board in your hands.

In the New Testament, it is different. The first representatives of the New Testament dispensation live and walk under a strong, almost inescapable impression of the fact that the end of the long series is close by, and day by day coming closer upon them. They live to a certain extent in the most vivid realization that the actual end is well-nigh present. Therefore they use the identical Greek phrase *eschatai hemerai* with somewhat of the sensation projected into it—that these Old Testament "latter days" were their own days and the final days. The English translators with a fine instinct felt this and reproduced the feeling in their translatorial minds by making the New Testament people say that they find themselves living in "the last days"; whereas, from a similar sort of projection into the Old Testament state of mind, they there render "the latter days." But this finely felt difference does not rest on a difference in the Greek original. It is the translator's instinct that has felt its way underneath and behind the phrase in accordance with the time and circumstances under which it desired to receive expression and under the guidance of inspiration.

Thus far, we have considered the reasonableness or the necessity of a finality-crisis and a finality-state purely from the standpoint of creation. But that world is a world of abstraction: such a world in the pure form of an unmodified, uncorrupted product of the creative act of God nowhere exists at the present. Taking the scriptural account as a whole, that state of the world, together with the potentialities or possibilities for eschatology that it might have afforded, lies far behind. The true practical way, therefore, of considering the matter is that which considers it from the standpoint of redemption. It will be noted that the intervention of sin, so far from destroying the underground of eschatology, has on the contrary imparted to it an altogether new and more intensified religious significance. What its supreme significance is we can only begin to measure when we ask what place it occupies in the world of redemption. For redemption is a divine procedure taking place in the form of time, in the form of history. Therefore, as such, it cannot be thought of without the implied idea of a terminus, a point of arrival. If an uncorrupted world already stretches itself out toward some goal of consummation, how much more will a creation fallen into sin and corruption. All the abnormalities, the uncomfortableness, the frictions and attrition of sin cry out for it. Paul has very strikingly described that state of mind by the figure of "groaning" (Rom. 8:22). Owing to the primordial sin of man, the whole creation groans, hoping to find deliverance from the bondage in which it is compelled to live as a result of the fall.

Now so far, this is only the pressure from man's dissatisfied subjective state; it is like beating at the iron bars of the cage. It becomes as intense as it is because through the bars, man is still, or let us say is again, enabled to see the paradise world of freedom and blessedness that surrounds his prison. For God has built the plan of redemption in such a way that it not only retains the principle of eschatological finality in it, but rather that it is for the first time all-pervasive, truly ubiquitous, something with which the whole prevailing religious order of things is shot through. The biblical redemption aims at a new creation and nothing less than that. Therefore, all the threads of purposeful finality are made to run together in the redemptive revelation of grace; all the rays of original eschatological light and splendor are refocused in it. The dignity of God as Redeemer postulates it and the truly pious soul will not, cannot, conceive of it otherwise. The promise reminds God of and, as it were, confronts him with the fact that he cannot abandon the works of his hands, that he must perfect what he has begun. This is but another way of saying that eschatology is the crown of redemption both from God's and from man's side.

Nor must we forget that it is not merely the extremely uncomfortable sinner who feels this way. There lies also in this the awakening or revival of the ultimate ideal of religious aspiration as such. The eschatological groaning of which Paul speaks, besides being a cry of pain on account of the misery of sin, has in it the undertone of an ineradicable desire for the complete, absolute possession of and satisfaction with God, such as within the present world is impossible. Hence the apostle adds: we ourselves, who have the firstfruits of the Spirit, even we also still groan within ourselves, stretching out praying hands of hope and faith toward the end (cf. Rom. 8:23). This is a longing, a prayer, a beseeching of God that only the redeemed subject of religion can experience. The groaning of the irrational creature is left far behind by it. The Christian alone can experience it and does experience it with such intensity that it became to Paul in itself a prophecy of fulfillment. It is like the craving hunger that knows there must be bread somewhere.

Individual and Collective Eschatology

Eschatology naturally divides itself into collective and individual eschatology. By the former, we understand what happens to the individual after death. Presupposing always that at some future point from that moment of death on, a further, comprehensive change will take place, a change affecting those who died before through a transition from the state of death, and in order to distinguish it from other individual experiences of change that may again take place, we call this first section of the state of departedness "the intermediate state."

The two phases of the subject, i.e., that called collective and that called individual eschatology, have something in common, but there is also much that is different between them. In Hebrews 9:27, a certain analogy is traced between what happens to the individual after death and what will happen at the end of the world: "Inasmuch as it is appointed for men once to die, and after this the judgment, so Christ also, having been once offered to bear the sins of many, shall appear a second time, apart from sin, to them that wait for him unto salvation." During the whole course of revelation in the Old Testament, collective eschatology has the preponderance, and to some extent this is still so in the New Testament. Only the relative difference in prominence is not so great in the New Testament as it is in the Old. But the main difference lies not in the bulk of this material; it lies in the far greater clearness and distinctness wherewith this side of the subject, highly mysterious in itself, is treated by the two dispensations. A veil hangs over the ancient opinions entertained, but likewise over the revelation-knowledge afforded as to the realm of the dead and the conditions prevailing therein. In objective eschatology, the difference is on the whole one between prophecy and fulfillment. In regard to the subjective side, it is a difference between ignorance or at best partial knowledge and the much fuller and clearer information consequent upon the coming of Christ and the completion of his work. This difference should be kept in mind in searching the Scriptures for eschatological detail in regard to certain points exciting the interest or curiosity of the investigator. It would be a perverse method to seek to prove from the Old Testament alone or chiefly that at the moment of death the pious Israelite went straight up to heaven. The uniqueness of the case of Elijah and the lack of explicitness in what is said about Enoch suffice to show how inadequate the content of Old Testament revelation is for that purpose.

Under this head it should be further observed that whatever progress was made during the Old Testament in clearness and fullness of the understanding of the issues of subjective eschatology took place in dependence on the clarifying of the issues of objective eschatology. Broadly speaking, in the Old Testament the trail does not run from the individual to the nation, but rather from the nation to the individual. This will appear in the following discussion of individual eschatology. In the New Testament, it is somewhat different. Individuals are won out of the Jewish church or out of the sphere of paganism and these, gathered together into one collective body or organism, impart, through their individual destiny, the characteristics belonging to the latter. Heaven is eternal because the believer united to Christ has received eternal life into himself. Something nevertheless has from the Old Testament method of procedure been perpetuated in the New Testament order of things; viz., that once the church has been formed, God deals not with the individual members constituting it as such, but with them and with their children. In that view of things, the collective organic principle is seen to assert itself once more. The Old Testament pious young man or woman was never regarded as not of the church, not even as only provisionally or hypothetically living in the environment of the church; the offspring in virtue of birth from church-parents formed part of the church *ab initio* ("from the beginning"). And this principle has passed over into the Christian church. The idea of "joining the church" is thus unbiblical and misleading in reality. It is God who joins, adds to the church; individual men or women do not join themselves to it by their own act. Such at least is the true principle where the church is antecedently established. In the sphere of missions, it must needs be otherwise.

We now pass on to the consideration of the so-called intermediate state. This is not, of course, a state or condition peculiar to the Old or to the New Testament. In both, people died and if anything was contemplated beyond at all, there was bound to spring up some conception of an intermediate state lying between. The trouble was, however, that it was difficult for the Old Testament people to see or understand that there actually was a clearly defined "beyond." Consequently, the idea of the intermediate state, while not absent, drew a great deal of the vagueness and indeterminateness of the entire knowledge concerning the future after death into itself. The land of enduring life was hidden in the mists of incomplete revelation, and for this reason the portal that could give admission to it stood in the shade, as stood the house itself. In order to get a correct conception of this condition under the Old Testament regime, we must carefully define the limits that had been set by God on the people themselves in this field. We must, moreover, remember that limits set for them in the sphere of knowledge in regard to their immediate postmortem experience are at the same time limits of knowledge and understanding for us when we endeavor to peer behind the curtain of their misty consciousness. Where the Old Testament consciousness abode in semidarkness, there, however much we may strain our eyes, we cannot easily get beyond a state of haziness in our own apperception. As Christians, of course, we know ever so much more about what awaits us than they did.

Yet at the same time as students after the most assiduous attention paid the subject, we, putting ourselves in their place, frequently feel that in that capacity of students or explorers, we know hardly more than what they knew in their own situation. We share, as it were, retrospectively in their ignorance. And yet this historical ignorance seems to have lent a peculiar charm to the endeavors toward clearing up the subject. It is a curious thing, but it is a real thing that there are Christians who feel more interested in the land of obscure fore-imaginings where the ancient Israelite abode, than in the luminous circle that has been drawn around us through him who has brought life and immortality to light. The story about the witch of Endor attracts and intrigues them almost more than the garden of the resurrection. That is an abnormal curiosity, all the more so because we are personally detached from the things then of living interest. Curiosity from the background of such detachments is a less healthy phenomenon than that exercised toward things that concern ourselves.

Now it behooves us, lest we fall into unbalancing extremes, to draw certain distinctions that ought to guide us in investigating or exploring or discussing these matters. What, then, are the principles that God has set up for dealing with the intermediate state for the Old Testament people? First of all, we must learn to distinguish between beliefs or superstitions on this matter, which had a wide, perhaps we should say, an almost universal currency among the people of those days and which they had received by age-long, immemorial tradition, and what they had learned through revelation. The former naturally constituted a great bulk, because that kind of knowledge is always apt to expand apace. On the other hand, the scanty material which revelation had up to their time been able to inculcate in them stems from the primitive character of the preparatory dispensation under which they lived. They stood under the *stoicheia tou kosmou* ("the first and beggarly rudiments of the world") as spoken of in Galatians 4:3 and Colossians 2:20.

Next we must try to ascertain what the average mode of contemplating the state of death and the state after death was among the people of the Old Testament. It is now in order to gather evidence concerning this matter from divine disclosures. (To whatever there was of the latter nature, I will revert presently.) On the whole it must be said that the general outlook on death was a dismal one. If it did not have the tragic character that belongs to it in certain pagan circles of antiquity, there was something of a high degree of gloom about it. While falling short of despair, it remained an even farther distance from positive joy than from despair. It might perhaps be characterized as a mood of resignation concerning that which could not be averted. It was of course in some way connected with religion, for there is no opinion or sentiment formed anywhere on such a subject in man's consciousness into which religion does not enter, no matter whether it be individual or collective eschatology that comes under consideration. It is difficult to gather from isolated utterances a clear and positive impression of how the pious (or the wicked for that matter) of the Old Testament regarded the mystery that lay before them and existed all around them, waiting, as it were, to draw them into its shadowy regions sooner or later. What we need is some book of Scripture that in virtue of its very purpose does revolve around this thought.

We are fortunate in having among the books of the canon such a writing in the book of Job. In this book the personages speak out of their own feelings. They speak moreover less didactically than poetically on the matter and on such a subject, not to mention many more. It is poetry that brings the deepest thoughts to light. Besides Job we have the Psalter, where the same conditions meet, although in the Psalter there shines through the more joyful sentiment of trust and even joy in view of the light that in later days God had granted his people in these concerns. It is interesting to observe that in Job the subjective attitude toward death that is reflected attaches itself not only to the friends of Job, but to Job himself. Now in order to make you feel what sentiment pervades this circle, I will quote a few passages from Job. In the third chapter, we are made to hear the following about the realm beyond death: "Why died I not from the womb, for now I would have lain still and been quiet, I should have slept" (3:11, 13); "He that goes down to the grave shall come up no more" (7:9); "I should sleep in the dust and thou shall seek me in the morning, but I shall not be (there)" (7:21); "I should have seemed as though I had not been" (10:19); ". . . the land of darkness and the shadow of death; a land of . . . darkness itself . . . without any order, and where the light is as darkness" (10:21–22); "But man dieth and wasteth away; yea, man gives up the ghost, and where is he?" (14:10); "O that thou wouldest hide me in the grave; that thou wouldst keep me in secret" (14:13); "For what pleasure has he [the wicked] in his house after him, when the number of his months is cut off in the midst?" (21:21).

12

From the Psalter, there might be added such passages as: "Return, O LORD, deliver my soul: O save me for thy mercy's sake, for in death there is no remembrance of thee; in the grave who shall give thanks?" (6:4–5); "What profit is there in my blood, when I go down to the pit? Shall the dust praise thee? Shall it declare thy truth?" (30:9) [30:10]; "He [the vainglorious wicked] shall go to the generation of his fathers; they shall never see light" (49:19) [49:20]; "I am counted with them that go down into the pit . . . among the dead, like the slain that lie in the grave, whom thou rememberest no more: and they are cut off from thine hand" (88:4–5) [88:5–6]; "Wilt thou show wonders to the dead? Shall the dead arise and praise thee? Shall thy lovingkindness be declared in the grave? Or thy faithfulness in destruction? Shall thy wonders be known in the dark? And thy righteousness in the land of forgetfulness?" (88:10–12) [88:11–13]; "Thou carriest them away as with a flood; they are as a sleep" (90:5); "As a flower of the field so he flourishes, for the wind passes over it and it is gone and the place thereof shall be known no more" (103:15–16); "The dead praise not the LORD, neither any that go down into silence" (115:17).

From the foregoing, it will appear what the common way of envisaging [the grave was]. . . . The question arises: Was this merely the ignorance or . . . [the lack of] . . . enlightenment among Israel in that time? Or was there . . . a dismal state of mind, be it a provisional dismal reality of [the future]? This question is not easy to answer. One thing is sure, we have no [right to] . . . generalize this conception of the state after death, as though it belonged to the fixed lot of the people of God for all generations, in the New Testament no less than in the Old. Our Lord through his teaching and resurrection has made this plain to us. After him and on the basis of his work, the apostles have made plain to us that of the present intermediate state such things can be, at least as to Christians, no longer affirmed. There has been progress not merely in knowledge in this matter, but a real change in the actualities of experience and destiny. But it would be rash to say that under the Old Testament the whole sphere of belief on this matter was a world of delusion. There must have been something corresponding to what was so deeply ingrained in the consciousness of Israel. Granted, it shows resemblance to the beliefs of pagan systems of religion in regard to such subjects; but that alone by no means suffices to discredit the objective reality of it. True, what the speakers in Job and the psalmists affirm and imply was not in the common sense revelation: it was the subjective utterance of their religious state of mind at various moments. It was not something that God through the expression of such despondencies desired to make known to us and that with the stamp of his absolute divine authority upon it. But it was not on that account withheld or withdrawn from the field of inspiration. Inspiration in such cases only vouches in an infallible way that such thoughts and misgivings and forebodings actually, and in that actual form, existed in the minds of pious Israel.

But the fact that in all this we conclude merely to the presence and operation of inspiration in that reportorial sense cannot prove that no realities and experiences and destinies existed at that time, such as justified for that time at least the sentiments of the people. In case this whole complex of belief had been merely a delusion and superstition of men, we might certainly expect that throughout these the general expectation with which the Old Testament people face death and the way in which they picture the state after death cannot be simply cast aside as a tangle of ignorance, error, or superstition. That some inadequacies of belief and expression of belief were mixed with it may be readily granted. But we have no right to assume this attitude toward the whole, and, carrying our richer and more adequate and more definite knowledge back into it, to force the meaning of the Old Testament utterances by a violent exegesis to make them say the same thing that we think they ought to say in order to cover our own knowledge. In case this whole world of beliefs and forebodings and dreads and expectations had been simply the product of human imagination, we might certainly expect that throughout the long record we have of the progress of revelation among Israel, some hints of correction or modification or of the necessity to shift the entire point of view should have been supplied by God. In any broad and comprehensive sense this is not done until relatively late.

Still there are exceptions to this generalizing statement just made. I cannot go into all the detailed material that might be gathered as qualifying more or less distinctly the rule laid down. But there are four passages in the Psalter on which I must briefly comment. The Psalms in which these occur are 16, 17, 49, and 73. Please take some pains to fix these references in your memory. In the first of these, Psalm 16:10–11, the psalmist expresses his confidence that Jehovah will not leave his soul to Sheol, neither will he suffer his holy one to see corruption. Many exegetes endeavor to reduce this to the idea that Jehovah will not permit Sheol to lay hold upon the singer—in other words, will not permit him to die. While the words in themselves are not incapable of bearing such a meaning, the true interpretation is different and we know it is the true one because it is vouched for by the quotation of the passage on the part of Peter (Acts 2:25–28). According to Peter, the words must be applied to the resurrection of Jesus. They express the conviction that God is unwilling to leave his servant, who is already in Sheol (or at least prospectively speaking will be in Sheol), under the power of death, but will on the contrary rescue him so as to make known to him the ways of life—to make him full of joy with his countenance and all this in such a way that meanwhile his flesh can rest in hope without becoming acquainted with corruption. The prospect of death has not been removed here, but the state of death itself has been transfigured and become a prophecy of glory. This is so appropriate to the resurrection of Christ that Peter's aptness in quoting it on the occasion is something quite extraordinary, a veritable stroke of interpretative genius. For, it should be remembered, the psalm is not in a direct, explicit sense a messianic psalm referring to Jesus alone. It enunciates a general principle, and Peter applies it to the one case in which it could find an exhaustively perfect fulfillment. Here is not only the life after death, nor merely the deliverance from what there is of death in this life; it is the divine victory of life over death in its highest potency.

As to Psalm 17, the psalmist draws a contrast between the wicked whose portion is in the present life (vv. 14–15), and who therefore, when taking leave of this present life must leave all their substance to their offspring; a contrast between these, I say, and the pious, specifically the speaker himself who is able to declare with assurance: "As for me I shall behold thy face in righteousness [i.e., in a state of full vindication], I shall be satisfied when I awake with beholding thine image [i.e., thy form]." It is not quite clear what exactly is meant by "beholding the face" of God and the attainment of satisfaction through the vision of the divine image, but the words are unique within the limits of the Old Testament and so striking that we need not hesitate to find here also the thought of the resurrection—all the more so since the figure of "awaking" enters into the representation and it would be hard to tell what they could possibly mean on any other basis than that of the resurrection-hope. In connection with this form of statement, attention should be called to the fact that in their collective eschatology, the Psalms sometimes speak of "the morning" in a fixed technical sense, meaning by it the break of the great light-filled Day of Jehovah. It is not impossible that the "awaking" should be intended to convey no more than that the psalmist's vision of Jehovah is thought by him so near as to make him interpose between it and the moment of speaking but a single brief night. Still, on the whole, this is not very plausible in the context (cp., however, "God shall help her and that right early"—Ps. 46:5 [46:6]), although in this statement likewise some expositors have found the figurative representation that the (eschatological) end will not be postponed long.

Psalm 49 works out the same contrast between the wicked that perish, compelled to leave their substance behind, and the pious singer. The wicked appear in the hereafter as a flock under the hand of Shepherd Sheol. Of himself, the psalmist declares: "But God will redeem my soul from the power of Sheol" (v. 15). This is followed by the words "for he will receive me," and these words prove that more than exemption from death is referred to. An act of God by which one already in the power of Sheol will be redeemed must be meant, but there is no further definition of what this act will be, nor of what the state or condition following this act of deliverance will consist in.

The fourth affirmation, that found in Psalm 73:23, 25, brings at least a partial answer to the point—easily the most momentous factor in the problem—for the psalmist declares: "Nevertheless I am continually with thee: thou hast taken my right hand: thou wilt guide me with thy counsel and afterwards receive me to glory." Although it may not be quite clear how this "glory" is conceived of, or what elements we may or may not include in it, it is plain that we have here a positive concept belonging to the sphere of beatitude. And somewhat more specific information, we receive even in regard to this in the statements of verses 25–26ff.: "Whom have I in heaven but thee and there is none upon earth that I desire besides thee; my flesh and my heart fail [i.e., although my flesh and my heart shall fail, not 'should fail'] God is the strength of my heart and my portion forever." These words in verses 25–26 establish a continuity between the pious intimacy with God in the present state and the experience of his favor in the hereafter. Not only is the psalmist's life, as it were, absolutely centered upon God, but God likewise in responsive attitude has shown himself to be the same. Because the psalmist has been continually with Jehovah and has been ever drawing closer to him, in this is found the assurance that such a relationship must be permanently secure. This passage represents undoubtedly the high-water mark of the confession of faith in regard to the intermediate state within the Old Testament. But, of course, it does not sharply distinguish between what comes immediately at or after death and the eternal fullness of glory that at some point after that may supervene. It is all compressed into one prospect. The deanalyzing of this again into its component elements had to await the further progress of collective eschatology both in the later Old Testament revelation and in the New Testament.

As to the date of these four psalms, it will be observed that in the titles Psalms 16 and 17 are introduced as psalms of David, and for the sixteenth we have in addition the testimony of Peter in Acts (cf. 2:25). The two other psalms are entitled for the "Sons of Korah" (49) and "a Psalm of Asaph" (73) respectively. The fixing of the time for the emergence of the faith they contain is, therefore, except in the case of Psalm 16, interdependent with the question of the dating of the Psalms in general and the weight which in that enquiry will have to be accorded to the titles. And this last is, as you know, a point of considerable controversy among scholars. Hence, I will not here reflect upon it any further.

From the Pentateuch one item of evidence must be added to these gleanings from the Psalter. It is found in Genesis 5:24 in the words concerning Enoch. As to what is said about him in Genesis 5, the following may be remarked. It is not related of him that "he died" as is affirmed of all the other members of the line of descent. The simple statement is "he was not." If this were imaginatively worked out, it would lead to the inference that he could not be found, that therefore his body shared in the removal to God. The words "God took him" by themselves hint at a new state of closer nearness to God. Now if the phrase "he walked with God," as it undoubtedly does, means more than that he led a pious life and refers to unique supernatural intimacy with God and initiation into divine mysteries, a parallel becomes noticeable between his life on earth and his state after removal. The walking with God and the subsequent nearness of God to him correspond. Notice that where God took him is not stated. The mode of statement in this respect remains within the limitations of the Psalter. Only the changed and intensified closeness to God, apart from more precise local definition, is stressed.

To this we may directly attach the brief report of what happened to Elijah, according to 2 Kings 2:9–11. The difference lies in the point that in the case of Elijah, we are distinctly told "Elijah went up by a whirlwind to heaven." The local point of arrival of the being taken by God is distinctly named. On the other hand, it is not so explicitly stated that it was God who took him. Elijah speaks twice to Elisha of his "being taken" or "being taken away from him" (vv. 9–10). Still the use of the verb *taken* seems reminiscent of the statement God "took him" in regard to Enoch.

Of Moses, who in later Jewish representations formed a trio with Enoch and Elijah in receiving the grace of removal without intermediate death, I will not speak in this connection. In the account of his departure in Deuteronomy 34, it is repeatedly stated that "he died" and was buried in a valley in the land of Moab. The only mysterious thing added consists in this: "No man knoweth his sepulcher till this day" (Deut. 34:6).

What was recorded concerning Enoch and Elijah was doubtless of extreme suggestiveness for the readers of these narratives. Herein lay germs of subsequent progressive revelation concerning the state after death. Only we must not go so far as to generalize the experience of these two heroes of the Old Testament faith in this particular direction that the event conveyed or was intended to convey to the Old Testament believers in the days when it happened and for which it was recorded, a comprehensive revelation concerning the state after death. This would be in contradiction with what we gather elsewhere about the beliefs of the people, even pious people. They doubtless thought such things happened to Enoch and Elijah, but were modest enough to reflect on the fact that not all of them were Enochs and Elijahs.

In all probability the Pentateuch contains still another witness to ancient belief in the state after death as subject to a degree of differentiation and not incapacitating a dead man for feeling happiness or distress. This is found in Numbers 23:10 in the first *mashal* of Balaam. Balaam exclaims: "Let me die the death of the righteous and let my last end [*acherith*] be like his." These *mashals* of Balaam are in several places and perhaps in their entire tenor eschatological. Israel has a quite distinct position and destiny with Jehovah. The result of this high status is described in terms of temporal, material blessedness. But in the verse before us, the seer, while enraptured against his own will by the vision of this happiness (he means to curse and is compelled to bless), reaches a climax by his reference to the death of the righteous or something connected with his death. Now the question is wherein precisely the blessedness consists that calls forth this eulogy. Some think that it is meant retrospectively, that the happiness consists in being at the moment of death able to look back upon a long life filled with the delights of prosperity and affluence, all of which was enhanced by the thought of the favor of Jehovah from whom all these things had come. This is possible because the Old Testament sets greater store by what may be called the temporalities of life, particularly religious life.

Still, this exegesis is not quite natural because the retrospect would take place at the point of death and with the unknown future entirely overlooked and ignored, the praise deriving its motive exclusively from the past would appear rather poor and overdone. The mere memories of the past could never entirely suppress the anxiety for the future and a future so close at hand at that. The other exegesis, viz., that which refers the felicitation to the desirable destiny that awaits the righteous after his end has come, finds its main support in the name given to him—*jeshurun*. Somehow what he is destined to obtain and his being "righteous" must have something to do with each other. That would be very important because it would introduce the principle of moral differentiation into the intermediate state: an unrighteous man would not obtain it, or would obtain something else. As it happens, however, the subject of whom this is predicated is not described by the usual adjective for "righteous" (*jashar*), but by the rare form *jeshurun*. And this is a proper name that is a couple of times used of the people of Israel, once in Deuteronomy (33:26) and once in Isaiah (44:2). This again points in the direction of finding, not an individual Israelite, but the people of Israel referred to in the whole verse. Everything would fit into this admirably, for the preceding context undoubtedly speaks of the nation. But here again arises the difficulty that, so understood, the statement involves the subjection of Israel as a nation to antecedent death before this happy lot can be accorded to it. The idea of the death of Israel has, so far as I know, no parallel in the Old Testament manner of speaking (except perhaps in Hosea and Ezekiel). You see how what may be said for and against either of the two views balances each other. The decision is thereby made very difficult. Personally, I incline to the individualistic interpretation. On the other view, it would also have to be asked what the speaker regards as the blessedness in store for Israel after he will have died. That would have to be restoration and prosperity after return from exile, but the question recurs again whether the Old Testament ever speaks of the captivity as the "death" of Israel. And, if one were to extend the prospect beyond that, nothing short of obtaining a national resurrection could be thought of. And this projection of the vision into the remotest eschatological future would not remove the unusual idea of a previous death of Israel which would have to be on this view of the matter something even more serious than the captivity.

Next we must examine in connection with this same subject (the Old Testament data on the intermediate state) the remarkable passage in Job 19:25–27—the passage most frequently quoted in discussions about the future life. The familiarity with and facile use of the words for practical purposes is no greater than the extraordinary difficulty of their interpretation. The words read in the English Bible: "For I know that my redeemer liveth, and that he shall stand at the latter day upon the earth; and though after my skin worms destroy this body, yet in my flesh shall I see God: whom I shall see for myself, and mine eyes shall behold, and not another; though my reins be consumed within me." This is the rendering of the Authorized Version (King James). I will now quote the Revised Version (American Standard Version) in order to show what changes it has introduced into the earlier translation. It reads: "But as for me I know that my redeemer liveth, and at last he will stand upon the earth; and after my skin, even this body is destroyed, then without my flesh shall I see God; whom I, even I, shall see, on my side, and mine eyes shall behold, and not as a stranger. My heart is consumed with in me." The RV further offers in the margin for "redeemer," "vindicator, Hebrew *goel*"; for "earth" in verse 25, "dust"; for verse 26: "and after my skin hath been thus destroyed, yet from my flesh shall I see God"; in verse 27 it puts for "even I shall see" the rendering "whom I shall see for myself"; finally in verse 27, the marginal reading substitutes for "my heart is consumed within me," "my reins are consumed within me."

The first change from "redeemer" to "vindicator" appears in the margin only; it is undoubtedly an improvement; a "redeemer" connotes a more particular conception, one who through the payment of ransom delivers another from bondage of some kind. The favor into which "redeemer" has come seems to be largely due to the rendering of the term and, for that matter, the entire passage by Jerome[2] adopted also by Augustine[3] which reads: "scio enim quod Redemptor meus vivit et in novissimo die de terra surrecturus sum, et rursum circumdabor pelle mea et in carne mea videbo Deum meum, quem visurus sum ego ipse et oculi mei conspecturi sunt et non alius; reposita est haec spes mea in sinu meo." Guided by this Luther simply renders: "aber ich weiss dass mein Erloser lebt, und er wird mich hernach aus der Erden aufwecken. Und werde darnach mit dieser meiner Haut umgeben werden und werde in meinem Fleische Gott sehen."[4] This translation is altogether much too free and linguistically unsupportable in detail, as you may verify by consulting any respectable commentary. Its *vitium originis* ("original defect") lies in the introduction of the term *redeemer*, which from early times until now has called up all the soteriological associations that cling to that title, and, besides being here inexact in itself, has forced unwarranted constructions and significations upon the sequel of the passage.

It is a great pity that in this way not only a strange element was introduced, but likewise that the thoughts that were intended have become obscured and some of them eliminated and that with this burden of misunderstanding the words have had to pursue their long and momentous passage through the ages. Careful reading of the context shows that "vindicator" is the name required by the situation out of which the passage grows. The situation is this—Job feels a sense of being persecuted on the part of his friends: "Why do ye persecute me as God . . . Oh that my words [i.e., the protestation of my innocence] were now written! . . . that with an iron pen and lead they were graven in the rock forever" (19:22–24). This shows that what Job proximately desires is vindication from the endless, wearying charges of his so-called friends. This is plainly expected by him through some interposition from God. What form this vindication will assume and in what condition when it comes it will find him and when it is over will leave him—that the sequel of the passage must tell, and in regard to that much depends on the rendering of verse 25b. And for determining that, again nearly everything is staked on the word *al'aphar*. Shall we here cling to the AV "he shall stand upon the earth" which, as stated, is also the text-rendering of the RV? Or shall we adopt the marginal translation of the Revisers? You will immediately perceive how important a difference this makes for the suggestiveness of the passage. "Upon the dust" reminds us inevitably of the grave: it represents Job as in the dust, as having died. And it is on this dust, the dust either of the soil of the grave or his handful of dust mixed with soil, that he is conceived as standing. What Job expects is that God after his death will proclaim from the surface of his grave, or from over the little remainder of his dust, that the right was on his side in the controversy with his persecutors. He will obtain for his satisfaction in this something far more impressive and enduring than the writing of the iron pen and lead, or the large monumental characters engraven on some conspicuous rock; viz., the vindicating verdict of God that none can efface or gainsay. Now the rendering "he will stand upon the dust" requires this, and insofar opens that little at least of an outlook into the world after death that it contemplates a vindication in that state. Such a vindication given under such circumstances could hardly remain a mere verbal vindication. We cannot help thinking in connection with it of some real consequences affecting the person of Job.

Let us turn now to the alternative "my vindicator shall take his stand upon the earth." While this does by no means rule out the possibility that it will address itself to the dead Job, it does not, like the other translation, positively require it: "the earth is, in distinction from the dust, the terra firma on which Jehovah will plant himself." This figuration of the scene contributes to the idea of its majestic character, forcibleness, and irrevocableness with which the divine vindicator will utter his sentence. By this we gain something and do not necessarily lose anything of the valuable suggestiveness of the other view, inasmuch as Jehovah from on top of the firm, solid earth can, with no less forcible effect, pronounce his verdict over Job dead than over Job still alive. Which of the two is meant the sequel and it alone must determine. Unfortunately, the sequel through its dark text is an inadequate guide, because it is next to impossible to make out what its obscure words mean. But in regard to the words already considered, let me add that the AV is almost certainly in error when it renders the adjective *acheron* in verse 25 with "at the latter day he shall stand upon the earth." The word *acheron* without more cannot possibly mean that; if it could and did, it would unmistakably refer the whole passage to the resurrection. *Acheron* fits perfectly into the figure of the "vindicator"; the representation that he stands as the last one upon the earth (or dust) signifies that he is the last one in the field or on the floor; the one who passes the decisive verdict that puts Job in the right, i.e., he has the last word.

Now, as to verse 26, the text is so obscure that I prefer not to make any attempt at explaining it. None of the commentators has succeeded in making out a reasonable sense of the whole statement, even though allowing himself the greatest liberties with the Hebrew words. The LXX gives no help. Fortunately, the closing words of the verse are plain and authenticate themselves through their connection with the opening sentence of verse 27. They are, "I shall see God" and verse 27 reads at the beginning: "Whom I shall see for myself, and mine eyes shall behold." You will observe that this introduces into the scene of the vindication the note of the satisfying vision of God. It is the profoundly relig-

ious element of the thirst evinced by Job for the supreme justification from God. This is stressed by the addition "for myself, and
mine eyes shall behold and not another [no matter whether the
last be taken as subject or object of the verb *I shall see*]." The one
phrase in the verse to which definite meaning can be attached
consists of the word *mibbesari*. This may mean two things, and
the sense you choose to give it determines to a large extent the
understanding of the entire situation. For *mibbesari* can mean
"from my flesh," which yields the idea that Job's flesh will be restored to him either through healing from his disease (i.e., in this
life) or at some point after death, which would mean his vindication at the resurrection. The other sense which the noun plus
the preposition is capable of bearing is "outside of my flesh," i.e.,
in a disembodied condition, after the disease will have stripped
him clean of his body. It would amount to saying: even in the
case of my death my vindication cannot fail to come. If we knew
for certain, or with any degree of plausibility, what the preceding
part of verse 26 means, it would probably enable us to make a
choice between "from my flesh" and "outside my flesh." But, as
I said, these words which precede are hopelessly dark. They are
rendered in the AV with "and though after my skin worms destroy this body, yet . . ." But neither "worms" nor "body" is in the
Hebrew, and the verb rendered by "destroy" is there in a hardly
recognizable and hence very dubious form. Under these circumstances, I prefer leaving this part of the passage entirely out
of account and will content myself with the minimum of the
two versions given to *mibbesari*, i.e., with the one that renders
"outside my flesh." In other words, I do not venture to find the
resurrection here, but at the same time must add that I feel a
certain degree of diffidence about this position. The resurrection may be there, but the unusual obscurity of a few words, perhaps due to corruption of the text, hinders us from outright
affirming it.

Next, we must briefly consider the role played by the notion
of the people "sleeping" after death in the consciousness of the
Old Testament. The narrative of the Old Testament is full of

this; "he died and slept with his fathers" is a quite common phrase, a sort of refrain as one look at your concordance will show you. The pessimistic passages in Job and in the Psalter are not infrequently quoted to support this view of the sleep-death (or "death-sleep"), but wrongly so, because some of them are too strong for that and would, if literally taken, point to annihilation or evaporation of the soul. When it is hyperbolically implied that God may come to look at his handiwork in Sheol and will be unable to find it, this does not suit the idea that the person concerned is sleeping in the ordinary sense of the word; for a sleeping person is not as a rule hard to find. Further details connected with this representation of the place and state of dead people in Sheol I must leave to you to gather for yourselves, because I wish to direct my attention and yours exclusively to the concept of "sleeping" itself. This is all the more important because the idea persists from age to age through Old Testament history and recurs with unbroken continuity in the New. Paul, no less than the writer of the Pentateuch, refers to such as have died as "sleeping" or "having gone to sleep" (Christ is firstborn of them that slept). Is this a figure? Figures of this kind we might make, but what has come down the ages and in a large circle of tradition was certainly not a figure originally.

There must have been a time, very probably lying far back of what the Old Testament relates concerning beliefs in Israel, when people literally assumed that burial meant for the dead entrance upon a state of sleep or somnolence, unaccompanied by consciousness or clear consciousness, and moreover not carrying the implication of some earlier or later awaking out of this state to the previous state characteristic of the life on the surface of the earth. Possibly the background or proximate source of such a literal construction of the terminology of sleeping was absence of the distinction between body and soul. What happened to the whole, undistributed man? The entire disposal of the dead man is therefore judged of from what is seen to happen to the body. Whether in that assumed ancient period a belief in annihilation prevailed as the correlate of the sleep-condition of the dead, we are no longer able to tell. A further reason for it being called a "sleeping" probably lay in the close resemblance of the looks of a state of ordinary sleep to the state and appearance of one laid in his grave. He had been put to sleep, or had been bedded in the earth. And just as to a sleeper under ordinary circumstances, so long as he is sleeping, no consciousness is ascribed, so in this ancient original use of the term, consciousness was not included in the imaginative picture formed of the dead.

So much for the primordial understanding of the representation. The pictures drawn from the Old Testament of belief in that time, taken even apart from revelation, have obviously left all this far behind. The element of unconsciousness has been eliminated. Whatever the dead are, befogged and benighted and wandering as in a dream, they are not, if one wishes to speak precisely, unconscious. This is capable of strict proof, and that not only with regard to the Old Testament state of belief, but likewise with regard to a far wider Semitic circle of religion. It ought to be noticed at the outset that what is said of the Old Testament dead is not exactly that they went to sleep or that they slept, but that they were laid out as a sleeper lays himself down to sleep (the word *jashab* not *jashen*, which is the specific word for falling to sleep or being asleep). Still, I would not make too much of this argument because *jashab* undoubtedly is very often applied to the movement of the body when a person bends down or drops down to enter upon the state of death. The main point, and a quite relevant point, is that while every *jashen* ordinarily involves a *jashab*, this cannot be simply turned around to saying that every *jashab* is a *jashen*. But, discounting this train of thought, it is clear that with the element of unconsciousness gone, the figure that originally owed its right of existence to that continued in undiminished use. People still thought and spoke of their dead as "sleeping." Some influence must be attributed in this to the power of inveterate habit. From times immemorial, the state of death had been called by that term. The terminology was not so easily laid aside for no other reason than that the newer associations had become different. For terms are in some respects more enduring and indestructible than the conceptions for which they originally serve as carriers.

Therefore, no valid argument from the sleep-terminology of the Old Testament ought to be drawn in favor of the formulated doctrine of a "death-sleep." Still, it is not altogether beside the point to add that mere inveterate habits of speech are scarcely sufficient to account for the phenomenon of persistence in this case. But what we should think of, besides that, to furnish us with a point of comparison for justifying the figure, is not so easy to tell. As a matter of fact, it was only just then growing out of the realistic stage into being a figure. The dead might be thought of in this stage of the development of the representation as "sleeping" because, no less than sleeping persons, they were existing without means of communication with the world of the living. The figure in this quite supposable case would concern only their relations to the living, not their mode of existence or their capabilities of thought and reflection on or among themselves. They would be as good as asleep in a sort of semi-awakeness from which it was difficult to rouse them by ordinary means, or even through extraordinary magical manipulations.

I should not like to go farther than this, but only affirm that at this early stage one of the points of comparison in the use of the figure lay in the expectation or conviction that in the same way as ordinary physiological sleep is usually followed by an awaking, the sleeping of the dead was so-called because there was expected an end to it, sooner or later, through a resurrection. For that, there would be not much of a solid basis in the Old Testament consciousness; the exceptions we have found in the Psalter and Job are sporadic and, moreover, somewhat enigmatic. Hence we are not at liberty to give them a regular constant place in the death-sleeping complex (regarded as a universally current way of speaking among Israel). What was positively found in it, or read into it, remains an obscure question. Perhaps, in addition to what has been remarked, we might still add that the state of the dead, while no longer now conceived as unconscious, could continue to be called a state of "sleeping" because of the haziness, the lack of form, the voidness and semi-emptiness with which it was pictured; or because it was thought of as an uncomfortable, dream-disturbed, tumultuous sleep. Let that be as it may, the main point to which our attention should be directed is not that. It is rather this: that the terminology about sleeping has obviously sloughed off the element of unconsciousness of the dead which in ancient pre-biblical times must have belonged to it. For affirmation there is ample and adequate evidence in the Old Testament writings.

Let me mention only a couple of facts. The story of the witch of Endor where, at the request of Saul, Samuel is made to appear, proves the belief on Saul's part in the continued existence plus consciousness of Samuel after the latter's death. For you will notice that Saul, in confidently expecting guidance or advice from Samuel, takes for granted that Samuel has not lost touch with the development of things in the relation of Saul, Israel, and its enemies. Saul perhaps thought it would prove a rather difficult thing to bring up from among the many common dead this eminent figure of Samuel, because there existed, as we will presently see, a sort of belief in rank or difference of distinction among the multitudinous inhabitants of the netherworld. For this reason Saul resorts to extraordinary means for bringing about what he desires, but all the same he cannot have thought it in principle impossible. It was only a question of more or less difficulty, and the behavior of the witch shows that her opinion was not much different on that point. Nor should it be objected to this line of reasoning that the whole narrative gives the impression that the transaction was disapproved of by God and presumably, on that account, also by the better minds of Israel. That is not to the point; for to assert that the thing was a forbidden practice is one thing; to say that there was no reality in it or back of it, that the whole was a fraudulent transaction on the part of the witch and a piece of gross superstition on the part of Saul, is not indicated by anything in the narrative. The narrator, whoever he was, certainly did not regard it so.

On this point as to the nonexchangeability of the two judgments that it was forbidden and that it was an empty phantasmagoria, we receive more light from a passage in Isaiah 8. The prophet denounces the desire of the people to obtain light on the political complications of the hour through intercourse with the inhabitants of Sheol. Their counsel is: "Seek unto them that have familiar spirits and unto wizards that peep and that mutter" (8:19). Jehovah opposes to all such practices the principle of the normal recourse in all religion; viz., to seek counsel from God and him alone—"should not a people seek unto their God? Should they resort for the living unto the dead?" (8:19). Here notice again that it is not the unreality or futility of necromancy that is condemned, but the substitution of such appeals to the world of spirits for the normal consultation of Jehovah, which is conceived of as taking place through prophecy. The possibility of following the other method implies that the dead are not unconscious. They make their power felt upon the wizards and the familiar spirits, but it is a forbidden practice into which Israel should not venture. Hence the injunction follows: "To the law [prophetic instruction?] and to the testimony: if they speak not according to this word, there is [there will be] no light in [for] them" (8:20).

In 14:4ff. of the same prophet, we meet the highly imaginative description of the manner in which the king of Babel will be received at his arrival in Sheol by the assembled kings he has, through his conquests, sent thither before himself: "Sheol is moved from its depths for thee to meet thee at thy coming: it stirreth up the dead for thee, even all the chief ones on the earth; it has raised up from their throne all the kings of the nations who shall speak and say unto thee, Art thou also become weak as we? . . . thy pomp is brought down to the grave . . . the worm is spread over thee and the worms cover thee" (vv. 9–11). Notice how here the dead kings are represented as weak in comparison with those which live on the surface of the earth, but they are not unconscious. They only need some stirring up to attract their attention to such an extraordinary event in the dull, shadowy routine of their lives as is the arrival of the king of Babel, whom they take pleasure in ironically greeting and reminding of his vanished superiority over themselves.

It is true the prophet speaks here imaginatively. His language is borrowed from the sentiment and mode of speech assumed by the Babylonians to be characteristic of Sheol, but there is no indication that he conceived of the Israelites as having different ideas on the subject. The "weakness" ascribed to those dwelling in Sheol, not excluding the kings of the earth, is significant of the antique conception of Sheol. Those dwelling there are not deprived of existence and they are not robbed of consciousness. They are only weak, like shades. Their attention to anything happening is dulled. They need stirring up. The difference between them and earthly creatures is sought not in the sphere of reality, but in that of activity. Like other functions, their consciousness may suffer impairment, but it remains clear enough to enable them to indulge in taunts and derision when they obtain the chance to vex their former oppressor. This whole representation is utterly inconsistent with the view that they were supposed to be sunk in sleep, which makes all distinctions disappear from the mind. And still one other feature is characteristic of this description: the kings assume a close connection between Sheol and the grave as the reference to the vermin covering the great king by way of an upper and nether bed-sack, as it were, indicates. The grave acquires the character of a vestibule to the regions of Sheol. References to this semifigurative way of speaking are found elsewhere also in the Old Testament.

The New Testament is very sober in affording information concerning the state of the dead. At first, this may seem strange because with the coming of the Messiah one would naturally expect that a flood of light would be let in on this subject. The expectation is only moderately fulfilled. Even so, however, there is more explicit and more abundant evidence than under the old dispensation. It is not inconceivable that the imagined nearness of the parousia which, of course, would introduce a totally new state of affairs with reference to which the old questions and riddles were bound to become largely irrelevant, had something to do with the phenomenon named. The following are facts that exclude the alleged unconsciousness in the intermediate state of the dead. Naturally, they relate to Christian dead. According to 2 Corinthians 5, Paul contemplates a possible death before the parousia, which would leave him in a state he would spend with the Lord. This of course cannot mean in the first instance the abode in the grave, although of the departed Thessalonians he affirms that they are *nekroi en Christoi* ("dead in Christ"), which does refer to the grave. But Paul envisages something beyond that; for he calls it a being with the Lord in absence from the body. Now of this contingent disembodied state (with the Lord), he affirms that there will be in it a certain degree of discomfort because, with the resurrection-body still lacking, one will feel naked. Such a feeling is obviously a self-reflexive state of consciousness (cp. with this Phil. 1:20ff., although there is no reflection here on the presence or absence of a body). But the implication of prospective joy in the nearness to the Lord is just as strongly affirmed as in the other context in 2 Corinthians.

As a third witness, we may place by the side of these Hebrews 12:22ff., where the author declares with reference to the then living Christians that they have come "to Mount Zion, to the general assembly and church of the first-born . . . and to the spirits of just men made perfect." This cannot be put to the account of an alleged spiritualizing trend of the writer because, according to 11:35, he was a thorough believer no less than Paul in the bodily resurrection. The fact of importance is that he depicts, in the passage quoted, a scene full of consciously experienced joy and light in the intermediate state for the departed believers of the Old and New Testaments. What is said about "the cloud of witnesses" encompassing the Christian at the time of writing is of the same tenor; for it certainly is not a purely rhetorical hyperbole. The scenes of the Apocalypse, where the martyrs are represented as crying to God from under the altar, may likewise be quoted here. But the most convincing argument, at least as far as Paul is concerned, lies in the analogy that he draws between the intermediate state of Christ followed by the resurrection and the experience in store for the believer.

It goes without saying that the apostle did not, nor could, conceive of the soul of Christ between his death and resurrection as sunk in unconsciousness and inertia. The picture of the descensus in Ephesians 4:8ff. is of the very opposite tenor: "When he ascended up on high, he led captivity captive. . . . Now he that ascended, what is it but that he also descended first into the lower parts of the earth?" The argument from the analogy of Christ's case is all the more stringent since Paul characterizes Christ as "the first-fruit of them that are sleeping." There is every warrant for saying that *koimasthai* as a figure for Paul moves entirely outside the sphere where consciousness and unconsciousness are relevant terms. How indifferent the term is by nature and tradition to any preference in settling the exact nature of the intermediate state, subjectively considered, may be perceived from this—it is not a specific biblical or special-revelation term. It is equally at home in the eschatological world of paganism, say Greek and Roman mythological and poetic representation. When the Roman poet says "nobis omnibus una nox longa dormienda est,"[5] the affirmation of unconsciousness lay far outside his intent of affirmation. He lacks even the association that was present in the New Testament and later Christian usage, viz., that every night is followed by a morn of awaking, because the words *una* and *longa* are chosen on purpose to express the thought that this is a single, all-engulfing, endless night. In other words, the figure of "sleeping" maintains itself even in the face of belief in utter extinction.

Where such philosophical or poetic agnosticism did not prevail, the representation of the condition in Hades involved, as little as the Semitic one, the idea of unconsciousness. There is speech and answer in Hades. Visits are received by certain outstanding legendary figures. Aeneas has a visit and interview with his father Anchises.[6] Achilles has a chance to express his disgust of the abode in Hades to the effect that a slave in the light of the sun is better off than a king in the lower regions.[7] All is shadowy and faint, redolent of poppies, "a sleepy world of dreams." But when these figures are pressed, the fact of retention of consciousness stands out in bold relief.

Now it is this point, consciousness versus unconsciousness, on which the interest in the controversy on this question is almost exclusively centered. This is particularly true of the modern survivals, or revivals, of this ancient opinion with which even now one may come in contact in the field of religious belief. John Calvin had his tilt of arms with it in the treatise published in 1534 entitled "Psychopannychia."[8] The treatise was directed against the Anabaptists who were zealously propagating the doctrine of "death-sleep." What precisely the animus and motive in this controversy were, on the side of the Anabaptists, I am not able to tell. Perhaps it had something to do with the desire for eliminating the conception of torment from the intermediate state, but this is just a pure guess of mine that I have not had time to verify. Suffice it to know that the doctrine has not emerged in the large current of Protestant doctrinal development. It bore then, as it still bears, a more or less sectarian character.

Collective Eschatology

We now pass on from the individual to the collective eschatology of the Old Testament. The idea of a future final destiny for mankind is from the beginning presupposed and often explicitly affirmed in the unfolding of biblical history. In order to gain a brief conspectus ("view") of the progress of revelation in this matter, we must first of all distinguish between the generally eschatological and the specifically messianic forms that the prospect assumes. Sometimes the approach and arrival of the end is ascribed to the supreme intervention of Jehovah, and nothing is said about the association with God in the future crisis of a secondary figure, usually called by us the Messiah. These representations are not, however, mutually exclusive even though they are not so closely knit together as to require in each case simultaneous expression. In some instances, they occur side by side in one and the same book of prophecy; e.g., Isaiah has them both. They have certain standing features in common: the supernaturalness of what they predict; the supernaturalness of the crisis introducing it; and the supernaturalness of the lasting state following. The most frequent term for the arrival of what is expected is the verb *to come*. This verb has outlasted the whole course of biblical process and still for us is the most convenient form of statement when we say that the Christ will come to perform his eschatological functions. But, while to us this manner of speaking has become largely appropriated by the messianic eschatology, and we speak far more of the coming of Christ than of the coming of God, it is different in the Old Testament dispensation.

There the expected advent of Jehovah is the generic idea out of which the specific notion of the coming of the Messiah in course of time is seen to develop. It ought further to be noted that the circumstances, the character of the coming, and the character of the conditions it introduces are dependent for their expression on the common medium of which the Old Testament revelation serves to express the happenings of religion. The eschatological forms of representation are not exempted from this. We must keep this in mind in our reading of the Old Testament eschatological scenes and not, simply because such a form is employed, draw the conclusion that the Old Testament has and teaches a time-conditioned and earth-complexioned final state. These forms were, in part, symbolic means of instruction and, in part, even required to be so understood from the first. To overlook these external media and forms of description and without preliminary reflection to throw ourselves upon them to translate them into spiritual values is not permitted. The root of much perverse interpretation of the Old Testament lies precisely here.

Still, on the other hand, you may say, perhaps in the interest of millennialism or of some other more or less materially disposed type of religion, that such a spiritualization is not allowable, that it opens the door to absolute arbitrariness of exegesis, that all that the Old Testament submits to us must be regarded as one and indivisible, that we must either take it as a whole or leave it as a whole. But it will be observed that we find the warrant for such spiritualization in the example of our Lord and his apostles. And not only this, we find a much earlier warrant for it in the Old Testament itself. The prophets themselves begin to see through the cover of earthly, material representation in which the institutions of the Old Testament were enveloped. The cover becomes to them a more or less transparent veil through which the spiritual essence underneath can be discerned and reveals to them its divinely created and innate beauty. Compare what Jeremiah says about the destiny of the ark. The ark of Jehovah is to be superseded in the eschatological period because in that era the sensual form through which its lessons were at first taught will have become superfluous. The knowledge of Jehovah and the forgiveness of sin, for exhibiting which the ark had first served as an instrument and a sacrament, will be more directly conveyed (Jer. 3:16; 31:31ff.).

Nobody has a right to say that the Christian church has falsified the Old Testament by spiritualizing it. The truth is that the prophets themselves began this transposition of things into a higher spiritual key, and the New Testament organs of revelation simply continued the process begun by them. When this is admitted in single isolated items, we should not deny the rightfulness of its being done on a comprehensive scale, for which also the New Testament offers the precedent. If it be said that the New Testament writers in this manner do not in all things sublimate the fulfillment, but that sometimes they point to single concrete items to which they ascribe the need of literal fulfillment, our business is not to generalize this into a vast system of repristination or perpetuation of the Old Testament forms of religion, but to study carefully the principle on which the Old and the New Testaments both proceed in their discriminating treatment of the eschatological material. Learn therefore from Peter and Paul this exegetical and theological secret. Do not handle the matter too much in the confusing details, but in its large, broad aspects. I say this with reference to both Romanism and premillennarianism, although it lies, of course, very far from me to identify these two systems.

First, then, let us enumerate the instances of objective eschatological disclosure in the Old Testament. The first redemptive revelation after the fall (Gen. 3:15) had this element in it because it predicted the final victory over sin, the removal of the curse, and, by implication, the return of the conditions of paradise. But already, the probation that preceded this had a very solid piece of eschatology in it because under the symbol of the tree of life it held out the prospect of a higher (i.e., the ultimate) life, which forms the goal of all eschatological revelation. The deluge was a type of the last judgment, as you may learn from the epistles of Peter (1 Peter 3:19–20; 4:5–6; 2 Peter 2:5; 3:5–7). The land of Canaan was a paradise-land in the typical sense; for it was a land "flowing with milk and honey" — the description, it seems, in the Oriental eschatological vocabulary, of the blessed future age.

The oldest form in which we can observe this generic eschatological belief in its unmessianic form is that of "the Day of Jehovah." We meet this in Amos 5, and not as a newly introduced element into the prophetic message. It appears as a commonly known popular belief, something to which the prophet can appeal. The people desired it because they expected from it only good for themselves or, at least, they expected if there was anything of an ominous nature in it that this would affect only the enemies of Israel, not the nation as a whole. At the utmost, perhaps they conceived of a cleavage within the nation and expected that the Day would strike only the wicked in Israel and not themselves. To each one of these perversions of the true import of the phrase, Amos takes exception. First, the idea is not to Amos an exclusively favorable one. It wears an evil face to his interpretation for he threatens, "Woe unto you that desire the day of Jehovah: it will be darkness and not light" (v. 18). Obviously, they had felt optimistic about it. But this optimism was not the only current view about it. There were others who did not quite share in this optimism and recognized that a measure of evil must needs be connected with the coming of this day. They realized that it boded little good, but while others had comforted themselves by stressing its light-character, they found the same relief through relegating it to a far distant time. According to 6:3, they put it far away, which of course carried the implication that the end that was coming would affect Israel not less, nay even more than, the other nations.

Notice the interrogative form in which Amos presents his warning: "to what end is it for you? It is darkness and not light" (5:18). The interrogative form, as well as the fact that they desired it, proves acquaintance with the conception on the people's part for a certain length of time in the past. And it is clear that it must have worn this double face already in the past. You will observe that as early as this the two principal aspects of the end of things appear side by side. Just as we say the end of all things will be judgment and salvation (or judgment and resurrection), so Israel of old affirmed the same two-sidedness: darkness and light were combined in their consciousness about it, although it seems that by some the two aspects were distributed over the two main groups of the people. Since that time, "Day of Jehovah" remained a fixed phrase in biblical eschatology. It passes over from the Old into the New Testament. Paul and the early Christians were just as familiar with it as was Amos. Isaiah (2:12; 10:3; 13:6, 9; 34:8; 61:2), Zephaniah (1:14–16), Joel (1:15), and Malachi (4:1, 5) carry on the tradition to the very end of the old dispensation. To be sure, afterwards, it becomes wedded to messianic eschatology. Hence in the New Testament it is sometimes difficult to tell whether "the Day of the Lord" means the Day of God or the Day of Christ.

But what is this "Day" and why is its character expressed in this form? There is much more back of this than the necessity of marking it as a definite, circumscribed event in the future. Various explanations have been offered. Some think that the figure is derived from the terminology of war. If one tribe secures a brilliant and decisive victory over another tribe, then the time of the battle used to be called "the day" of such and such a tribe. In that case, we should have a borrowing here from the secular sphere. Thus, we read in Isaiah 9:4, "For thou has broken the yoke of his burden, and the staff of his shoulder, the rod of his oppressor, as in the day of Midian." Only this illustration is not entirely satisfactory, for the day of Midian is not the day in which Midian comes off victorious. On the contrary, it is the day in which he is defeated. Next, it has been suggested that the origin and meaning of the phrase are derived not from the military sphere as such, but from that sphere in its religious aspect. It would then designate the day in which Jehovah is the one sublime, glorious figure standing out above all others that are with or arrayed against him in the battle. The day, as it were, monopolized by Jehovah, as in a different form Isaiah expresses it in chapter 2 of his prophecy: (in the midst of the earthquake that levels everything to the dust) Jehovah alone shall be great (vv. 2–5).

The fault with these explanations is that they find in the word *day* no more than a definition of time. There are indications that this word has a content and associations lying apart from chronology. The probability is that it meant, at least originally, the day as a season full of light, the day that in its breaking forth chases the darkness away. That is the reason why Amos's hearers evidently could scarcely think of it otherwise than an occasion that boded good for themselves. For did its very name *day* not presuppose this? The prophet corrects this unwarranted assumption, but does not mean thereby to reject the inherent meaning of the phrase as signifying the light-appearance of the eschatological crisis. It is and remains light, but in the first place light for Jehovah and darkness for the sinners in Israel. The figure has put its impress upon the New Testament representation that the parousia, the "coming" of Christ, is at the same time an epiphany, a "shining forth." It plays a large role in the prophecies of Isaiah (the second part of the book). It has received a peculiar turn through Paul who, in two contexts (Rom. 13 and 1 Thess. 5), has made the contrast between the night of the pagan life and the nearness of the daylight for the Christian the occasion for exhorting his converts to live in a manner comfortable to the day-time when even the wicked restrain themselves from a sense of shame. He also draws from it this further lesson that the Christian should be eschatologically awake, living as though the light of the near coming of the Lord were already enveloping him.

In these passages, it is very clear that to Paul the word *day* in "day of the Lord" and "the light" idea were closely grown together. Even the darkness of the pagan world is in these passages not a mere figure for the corruption of the pagan world in general. It is a figure eschatologically colored. The world throws itself headlong into all excesses of wickedness because it is obsessed by a desperate sense of the speedy approach and the inevitableness of its doom. The world makes all the use possible that this night of dissoluteness affords it; for it reasons, "Let us eat, drink, for tomorrow we die." The world lives, as it were, in a kind of cosmical night-club, whereas the Christian should pursue the last things to be attended to before the break of morning, "and that knowing the time, that now it is high time . . . for now is our salvation nearer than when first we became believers. The night is far spent, the day is at hand, let us therefore cast off the works of darkness and let us put on the armor of light. Let us walk honestly, as in the day; not in rioting and drunkenness, not in chambering and wantonness" (Rom. 13:11–13). And in Thessalonians: "But ye brethren are not in darkness in that that day should overtake you as a thief; ye are all the children of the light and the children of the day; we are not of the night; for they that sleep sleep in the night, and they that be drunken are drunken in the night" (1 Thess. 5:4–7). Here it will be observed Paul has pressed into the comparison still another element; viz., the element of vigilance. There is probably in this passage a reminiscence of the parable of our Lord about the wise and foolish virgins (although there "preparedness," not "vigilance," is the real point of comparison).

For the remainder, still confining ourselves to the nonmessianic forms of statement, there is no single concept that could be put by the side of that of "the Day of Jehovah." The regular form used to describe the great thing that is coming is the language of the theophany, the appearance of God upon the world-scene. The imagery employed to describe this, or rather to depict it, is exceedingly rich, but it remains in this general pictorial form—which does not mean, of course, that it meant to those who first looked at it or continued to mean a mere figure to be diluted and translated into other spiritual terms at will. The Old Testament people were poor translators, by no means experts in that line. It is only Jehovah who translates easily and perfectly because he finds himself the motif and the spirit of what these variously described scenes are to reveal when the fulfillment comes. The imagery of tempest and earthquake and thunderstorm and flood are all called into service for heightening the impression. Only the figure of the volcanic eruption is, among all these figures, of non-Canaanitish origin; for, so far as we know, volcanoes never existed in Palestine (which feature incidentally adds one more proof to the evidence for the ancient origins of the eschatological revelation and belief). As to the flood, the figure of this is handled in obvious dependence on the account of the deluge. In Psalm 93, Jehovah's control of the primeval flood is typical of his action at the future eschatological flood: "the floods have lifted up their voice, O LORD" (Ps. 93:3a). That relates to the past deluge, but the second part of the verse relates to the future counterpart: "The floods will lift up their waves" (Ps. 93:3b). But notice that the waters of Noah are not the only waters of eschatological significance in the Old Testament. When we come to look at the Psalter, we will find there the waters, the streams that make glad the eschatological city of God (Ps. 46:4).

It will be observed that so long as the prediction clothes itself in nature-images and nature-language, it remains in a certain sense independent of the time-prospect that must intervene before the judgment comes. Violent eruptions and upheavals of nature are not subject to calculation. They can be conceived nearer or farther off. There is no telling which of the two will actually prove to be the case. The prophetic eschatology, however, makes use also of the military framework in which to paint the judgment. For instance, the Assyrian attack upon Judah and Jerusalem in the eighth century B.C. will result in a great supernatural act of deliverance. Prophecy not seldom puts immediately behind the occurrence of such an epochal crisis, not the provisional resumption of the average, normal course of affairs as it existed immediately before, but delights to foreshorten the perspective so as to make it appear as though so soon as the proximate crisis is overcome, the final glory will burst upon the people. Later on it then sometimes is enabled to see that the intermediate plain that lies between its first great disclosure and the mount of consummation contains in itself a number of additional crises. The blank foreground originally overlooked divides itself into a succession of repeated occasions for winding up the process. These are the little hills between, apt to be overlooked when the eyes are fastened upon the supreme summit closing up the horizon. The ordinary, unprophetic way of reading such a prophecy cannot help being more or less misleading. Thus, in the Assyrian crisis described in Isaiah 28–33, the reader several times finds himself translated out of the turmoil of Zion's war into the ideal conditions of the restored newness of paradise. Compare, for example, Isaiah 29:17: "Is it not yet a very little while, and Lebanon shall be turned into a fruitful field, and the fruitful field shall be esteemed as a forest?" And "in that day shall the deaf hear and the eyes of the blind shall see out of obscurity and out of darkness" (29:18).

The nature-element in such descriptions is not entirely accounted for by putting it into the rubric of symbolic painting. It occupies in its very capacity of nature-makeup an indispensable place in the coming world. Through the extreme, one might say the one-sided, exclusive emphasis that the critics of the Wellhausen school have placed upon ethical preaching, they have been driven into the position that the great ethical prophets could not have attached any importance whatsoever to nature, either so far as nature-catastrophes or the resulting nature-products are concerned. The world-crisis at the end cannot, according to these men, have appeared to the prophets as coming about in any supernatural way. Notice they say not only that such things are impossible from their own standpoint, but they attribute the same standpoint to the prophets themselves. Hence the nature-elements fall for them under suspicion of spuriousness. They were added by redactors in subsequent times. Nor is it only their antisupernaturalism that speaks in this. Much also is in this conclusion the result of their Pelagianism, that is to say, in the interest of pure ethics and free will, they exclude the principle of free grace as having in any wise molded the eschatology of the prophets. This verdict is, however, restricted by them to the great prophets in their virginal period. Afterwards, when foreign influences streamed in from the Orient, the character of prophecy changed. It became apocalyptic. The beginning of this is found in Ezekiel.

But in this point also the Babylonian investigations have brought to light that such a view taken of eschatology is pure abstraction. If the Old Testament borrowed from the Orient at all, it must have had room for and interest in the transformation of nature. The view criticized is not "Ethics." It deserves the name of "Ethicism." It represents a mutilated, emasculated eschatology. That is to say, it is no eschatology at all. The promise received by the prophets and handed on by them to subsequent generations of Israel is to the effect that Jehovah will create a new heaven and a new earth (to be sure, one in which righteousness shall dwell, but yet a new heaven and earth—Isa. 65:17; 66:22). The apostle Peter did not think that this all-comprehensive cosmical promise was in any sense exclusive of its ethical correlate; for in quoting the phrase "new heavens and new earth" from Isaiah, he adds "in which righteousness shall dwell" (2 Peter 3:13). That is the normal Christian attitude. To get the new spiritual world without its proper physical milieu and environment to subsist on is contrary to the entire tenor of the biblical eschatology. It would amount to a doctrine about the resurrection without a resurrection body. The Old and New Testaments both place a well-proportioned emphasis on the body as essential to the integrity of human nature in the same way and for the same reason, without inclusion of the natural world in its scope.

The one specific part in this objective eschatology that receives specific attention in the Old Testament is the prediction of the resurrection. This occurs, besides the passage in Job already considered, where some find the idea of the resurrection and others not; i.e., in two contexts (Isa. 26:17ff. and Dan. 12:1ff.).

Observe that in both passages, the mention of the resurrection arises from the dark background of oppression, God-forsakenness, a sense of religious futility (this in Isaiah), and yet in contrast, as a sort of recoil from this, there springs not merely the hope, but the positive assurance of the resurrection. The resurrection must restore. This is the vindicatory significance of the resurrection meeting us still in the New Testament. Notice further in this same connection that the arrival of the great turning about of things is not expected by the people from their own self-willed exertions: they were with child; they were in pain; they brought forth nothing but wind, wrought no deliverance in the earth, neither could they cause the inhabitants of the earth to topple over. Besides, the Isaianic passages are peculiar in that they bring the resurrection into direct connection with the future eschatological state of blessedness following it. Going back in Isaiah to 25:6, we read: "and in this mountain will Jehovah of Hosts make unto all peoples a feast of fat things, a feast of wines on the lees, of fat things full of marrow, of wine on the lees well refined." Still further in this place there is the note of universalism that is not present in Daniel 12. For the prophet goes on "and he will destroy in this mountain the face of the covering that covereth all peoples [note the plural], and the veil that is spread over all nations. He has swallowed up death forever; and the LORD Jehovah will wipe away tears from all faces" (v. 7). This prophecy in chapter 25 differs precisely from the passage in the following chapter in that it strikes this note of universalism, whereas in the other context the significance of the resurrection for Israel is brought out. You see how dangerous it is to conclude from single, isolated statements to a partial, preliminary resurrection on the chiliastic (premillennial) principle.

As to Daniel, here we have a partial resurrection brought into view, for we read that "many of them sleeping in the dust of the earth shall awake" (Dan. 12:2). At the same time, this is a two-sided resurrection because it is added, "some to everlasting life, and some to shame and everlasting contempt." Of the resulting condition and state of the former class, only this is said: "and they that be wise shall shine as the brightness of the firmament . . . as the stars forever and ever." To say that this fixes for the entire future development of the doctrine the principle of a preliminary resurrection at the opening of a premillennial period is to confound the partial disclosure with the partial, numerically limited embodiment of the idea into facts. The passage does not deny any universal co-temporaneous resurrection. It only stands at a juncture when the process of revelation had not yet reached the point where the comprehensiveness of the principle was ripe for disclosure.

Relation between Eschatology and Messianic Prophecy

Eschatology is the genus of which messianism (messianic prophecy) is the species. Hence, all messianism is eschatological, but not all eschatological forecasts are messianic. As a matter of fact, the two terms have been used indiscriminately, which was at first excusable on account of insufficient elaboration of material, but now has become misleading.

The various types of eschatological representation in the Old Testament showing the place occupied by the messianic type, strictly so called, are as follows. (1) The generally eschatological type as a formal representation in which no human figure appears. In a theophany, Jehovah himself will impose and usher in the new order of things. "Jehovah's coming" and the absence of a human figure distinguishes this type from the three below. (2) The combination of a human figure with Jehovah, with both "to come," but the human figure is not a specifically royal character. (3) The combination of a specifically royal figure with Jehovah. The royal human figure is not distinctly associated with the theocratic dynasty of David, for the conception of a royal Messiah antedates the historical kingdom of Israel. (4) The combination of a specifically Davidic royal figure with Jehovah in such a way that the human figure enters into organic union with the Davidic line of kings. This type shows how much the Messiah has been associated with the Israelitish royalty.

Strictly and etymologically speaking, we can only speak of a Messiah as that presented in the fourth type. The first type is strictly eschatological and the remainder messianism. One will find these distinctions side by side in one author, i.e., Isaiah. Thus, since the name *Messiah* is derived from the anointing of the historic kings, it would be logical to restrict the title *messianic eschatology* to the fourth type.

In the postcanonical period, the messianic figure is absent or obscured. This is due to two factors. (1) The idea of Messiah became extremely human and strangely the eschatological idea became more transcendental. Therefore, the son of David seemed less capable of occupying the messianic place. (2) There was the auspiciousness of the Maccabean age which was looked upon as possibly messianic; yet the Maccabees were not Davidic.

Next we will discuss the etymology and import of the term *Messiah*. Etymologically, "Messiah" is from the Greek transliterated form *Messias*. The latter is from the Aramaic *Mashicha'*, which corresponds to the Hebrew *Mashiah*. These passive forms are derived from *mashah* ("to anoint" with oil). The form is an adjectival one, not a passive participle. As such, it is expressive of a lasting quality as a result of the act of anointing. The participle, on the other hand, refers only to the act and describes a single period of anointing.

According to Lagarde, the term *Messiah* comes from a Nabatean form *Mishshiha*, with an active meaning signifying "the anointer."[9] His two linguistic arguments are: (1) the Nabatean form affords an explanation of the *e*-sound in the

Greek form, i.e., it derives from the *i* in *Mishshiha* and not from the *a* in *Mashiah*; (2) the doubling of the sibilants (-sh) is not found in the Hebrew form. Against this, we observe the Greek transliteration sometimes changes the *a*-sound into an *e*-sound (cp. *Jephies* [LXX] for *Japhia* in 2 Sam. 5:15). Sometimes the Greek duplicates the *s*-sound of the original (cp. *Jessai* for *Jishai*). And second, the versions all render the word passively (Christos—LXX; Unctus—Vulgate; so too the New Testament—cf. Acts 10:38). The Old Testament eschatology never presents the Messiah as an anointer (active sense), i.e., communicating the Spirit within the Old Testament. In the New Testament, we first meet with this idea, but is it not called "anointing." The New Testament speaks of "baptizing with," "bestowing," "pouring forth," etc. the Spirit, but never as an act of anointing on Messiah's part. First John 2:20 suggests the idea of "anointer," but many exegetes hold that God is here the subject.

Who are the recipients of an "anointing" in the Old Testament? "Messiah" is used in the Old Testament in reference to the high priest in Leviticus 4:3, 5, 16; 6:15 (Hebrew, 6:22 EB) as an adjective and in Daniel 9:25–26 as a noun. In certain laws, other priests are also "anointed," but the title is reserved to the high priest. The theocratic king is called "the anointed of Jehovah" (note the construct state with Jehovah, God of Jacob, i.e., "My anointed"; the absolute form never occurs). It is also found referring to the patriarchs (Ps. 105:15 = 1 Chron. 16:22, metaphorically = "sacrosanct"). Cyrus is called the "anointed one" (Isa. 45:1). The phrase is often applied to the central eschatological figure (next to God): 1 Samuel 2:10; 2 Samuel 22:51 = Psalm 18:51 (50 EB); Habakkuk 3:13; Psalms 2:2; 20:7 (6 EB); 28:8; 84:10 (9 EB); 89:39 (38 EB), 52 (51 EB); 132:17. It is often disputed whether the Messiah ever occurs in the Old Testament with application to the eschatological king. In some of these passages, recent exegetes find a reference to the nation of Israel as "the anointed of Jehovah." Now it is the question whether the eschatological king is Messiah or not. Wellhausen and others apply these references to the people and, when a king is mentioned, to a dynasty.[10] This rules out the Messiah as a person and this is, of course, the important question. It's a question whether the Psalms had shaken off this figure of Messiah. The term *Messiah* is never applied to the prophets in the Old Testament. As an ordinary priest, he was anointed, but was never called "the anointed."

There are two major theories on the relation between the priestly and royal anointing. The view of Stade is that the priestly anointing is the older of the two.[11] From it, the king-anointing developed. Thus a priestly element was added to kingship; or, the king's anointing was supposed to confer priestly privilege. Wellhausen holds the opposite, i.e., that the royal-anointing is the older of the two. From it the (high)-priestly anointing sprang. Originally, induction into the priestly office was not by anointing, but by "filling the hand" (*mizze' iaad*). The later laws retained this idea, but added anointing. In older times, there is no reference to priestly anointing (yet one does read of it being wicked to slay a king because he is the "anointed one"). Zechariah 4:14 refers to Jeshua and Zerubbabel and is the oldest reference to "anointed ones." Wellhausen further believes that Jeshua allowed himself to be anointed as head of the congregation by applying to himself a kingly ceremony. He was therefore virtually king. And from this time the high priesthood is virtually a royal position in Judaism. Wellhausen explains the "filling of the hand" as the first payment of induction into office.[12] Later laws did not understand this and described it as the placing of a wave offering before Jehovah upon the hands.

Wellhausen's view may be criticized on the following grounds. First, in Judges 17:5, Micah applies the process of installation to his son and there we would scarcely expect him to pay his son on becoming priest. Second, if it meant the paying of wages, we scarcely expect this to apply to the priest. Wellhausen says only the priests were paid. Micah 3:11, however, reproaches the priest for receiving payment. Third, that it started with Jeshua after the exile is hardly probable because we would not expect it as long as the royal position was held by

Zerubbabel. Finally, on this view, how did other priests come to be represented as anointed?

There is an element of truth in the view of Stade. Certain considerations favor the idea that the king participated in priestly affairs. Still, it cannot be said that this was derived from the anointing of the king. David danced before the ark and was dressed in a priestly garb (2 Sam. 6:14). David and Solomon blessed the people, a priestly function. In the royal sanctuary the priests seem to have been servants of the king, and the kings exercised priestly prerogatives. This argument, however, cuts both ways and sheds no light on the priority of the one over against the other. The anointing of the king was performed by the priest. Jehoiada was chief actor in making Joash king (2 Chron. 23:16–24:16; cf. 2 Kings 11:17–13:19). Sometimes this function was exercised by the prophet—Samuel anointed Saul, for example. It might seem that this priestly anointing took place to impart a priestly character. (It foreshadows the intimate union of the two functions in Christ, which is also predicted in the Old Testament.) This priestly character, however, is not derived from the anointing as such. Psalms 2 and 110 suggest that anointing is king-anointing; perhaps this is due to the predominance of the Messiah-idea. The better view, on the whole, is to find in the two anointings, that of priests and kings, concurrent customs. The Messiah's anointing is more closely related to that of the kings.

The preceding discussion raises the question—was the theocratic king regularly anointed? Some hold that the ceremony belonged to the kingship as such and took place at each new accession to the throne. Others hold that it was not the rule, but the exception, applied only either where the new king was the first out of his family or where there was more than one claimant to the throne. All cases of anointing mentioned happen to belong to either the one or the other of these categories, but the argument is inconclusive because there also happen to be only cases where induction to office is described in detail. The significance and content of the royal anointing makes the first view the correct one because the king is regularly called "the anointed of Jehovah" (Judg. 9:8; Lam. 4:20). Anointing places a stamp upon the king as a uniquely appointed person of Jehovah. In fact, "the anointed of Jehovah" is a generic name and is almost identical with "king." Judges 9:8 says that the trees went out to anoint over them a king. Lamentations speaks of the "anointed of Jehovah" (4:20). The emphasis lies not with the declaration, but in the appointment to the office. Still, this is not necessarily the main thing.

Through anointing, a unique relation with Jehovah is received. Such a person receives a unique sanctity and a supernatural influence owing to a close association with Jehovah. Consider the following: (1) murder of the king is terrible and equivalent to touching Jehovah (cf. 1 Sam. 24:6; 26:9); (2) cursing the king was placed on a par with cursing God (cf. 1 Kings 21:10ff.); (3) in "the anointed of Jehovah," the genitive is possessive (i.e., in a peculiar way, Jehovah's), rather than one of authorship. (The peculiar king-reverence was not based on patriotism, but religion. The joining of these two elements, i.e., the unique relation to God and special reverence, is intensified in Christ.) Finally, a concrete supernatural something has been communicated to the anointed one. Some say the oil or fat represents the finest element of life and of this the anointed ones were the recipients. But among the Israelites it soon began to be connected with the Spirit of Jehovah. Zechariah 4:6–10, 1 Samuel 11:6, and 1 Samuel 16:3 tell us that he shall come to power by the Spirit of Jehovah. This intimate relation with the Spirit is seen in the metaphorical usage of anointing in the sense of bestowal of the Spirit (cf. Isa. 61:1). James 5:14 alone speaks of a literal anointing. Christ in the New Testament is not only the "anointed one," but the bearer of the Spirit. This points out the christological importance of anointing. To sum up, royal anointing involves: divine appointment; divine relation and reverence; divine Spirit.

We append here a note on the origin of the abbreviated form "the Messiah" out of the original fuller form "the Anointed of Jehovah." Dalman suggests that it was due to the Jewish custom of scrupulously avoiding the pronunciation of the divine name, Jehovah.[13] This was characteristic of the later Jews (but cp. Pss. Sol. 17:32; 18:6, 8; 2 Bar. 39:7; 40:1; 72:2; 4 Ezra 7:28; 1 Enoch 48:10; 52:4; Luke 2:26, possibly also 2:11).

2

PAGAN ESCHATOLOGIES

We first make the following general remarks on this topic. Eschatology is not found in pure nature religions because these rest on the unending round of natural processes knowing no development or goal. Eschatology is hardly conceivable since the end of the natural existence of things (which eschatology suggests) would necessarily involve an end of their belief (because the object of belief would be annihilated). There is here virtually no eschatology since nature is dependent upon a series of repetitions. Should these cease, nature ceases and with it belief ends.

Eschatology is a possibility in a higher type of nature religion, i.e., the mythopoeic varieties. These believe that nature has been subject to great convulsions and catastrophes in the past. This pattern is, of course, subject to repetition in the future. The idea of a beginning may beget the idea of an end. Thus, where the past is injected into the future, we find an eschatology among the pagans. More particularly, eschatology, although it became in its ultimate form one of the most distinguishing features of the revealed religion of the Bible, should not be understood as something confined to the biblical circle of religion. It is not in its whole extent a product of special revelation, nor of special grace exclusively. Because it is in its biblical form something so

53

unique, so distinguished, so profound, we are perhaps overinclined to deny it in toto to the pagan world. This is not correct. In various quarters of the world outside the circle of the true religion there was something to which the name of "eschatology" cannot be denied. The important thing is not to deny it, but to observe all the more sharply the respect in which it differed from the scriptural product.

We find this pagan eschatology among the Babylonians, the Egyptians, and the Persians, as well as in Hellenistic syncretism and the Roman sphere of belief. The expressions of it in these various quarters are so much alike that they almost compel us to assume that a general, widely prevailing background of eschatological belief or superstition was underlying it. This primitive eschatology had its own technical forms and formulas, and these were put to use where in some solemn situation strong language was required. All sorts of strange things were fabled concerning a king: his extraction, his nature, the prospects, as we would say, of his rule. That is not eschatology in itself. It is the vocabulary of eschatology put to outside use. "The King lives forever" is a phrase belonging to this realm of what you might call literary or court-ceremonial eschatology.

When we go back of that and compare the pagan analogies of "things heading for an end," etc., with the biblical teaching, we soon perceive the fundamental idea in which they differ from the scriptural teaching on the subject. They are no real eschatology at all, simply because the end toward which they represent things as heading is not an absolute end, but the concluding segment in an unrolling sheet of world history which, when once read, gives place to another sheet. It is world after world, cycle after cycle, with no perceptible termination. The thing is best known to you, no doubt, in the ancient idea of the successive ages of gold, iron, brass, stone, etc. The Babylonians derived this pseudo-eschatology from astronomical, or better, astrological observation. Their sky-readers had observed that at the point of the spring equinox, the figure of the ram in the Zodiac occupied in the course of time a more advanced position. Obviously, this was not a question of observation for two or three years. It required ages and carefully kept records. Now it was easily perceived that if this went on with the customary astral precision and inevitableness, it required only sufficient duration until the sign should have made its journey around the whole circuit of the Zodiac and, returning to its point of departure, conclude the course of what they considered a cosmical year. Such was their eschatology. It did not take its departure from God, but from the creature, which is symptomatic of all pagan religious development. You can even now catch the least little bit of an echo of that in the beautiful Christmas hymn, "It Came Upon a Midnight Clear":

> For lo, the days are hastening on
> By prophet bards foretold,
> When with the ever-circling years
> Comes round the age of gold;
> When peace shall over all the earth
> Its ancient splendors fling,
> And the whole world give back the song
> Which now the angels sing.

The "age of gold" is, in that form of naming it, not the enduring age; it is not the age of eternity to which Christian eschatology looks forward. It is one edition of the cyclopedia, not the unwritable book of God's composing.

Egyptian eschatology is based upon four texts which are said to have been found and to have been written ca. 2250–2000 B.C. The unwritten form is said to be much older (ca. 3750–3000 B.C.) Papyrus Golenischeff is a prophecy written by a priest under King Snefru (ca. 2000 B.C.).[1] It presents the contrast between a time of great convulsions and tribulations such as robbery, invasion, famine, solar disturbance, etc., and a period of great salvation and blessedness in which truth, prosperity, victory, etc. will be rampant. The change from the former to the latter will be brought about by a king from the south, born of a woman and a

"Son-of-Man." The Leyden Papyrus contains the admonitions of an Egyptian sage (ca. 1300 B.C.).[2] Here too, the contrast is between a period of calamities and a following one of refreshment. The latter is brought by a "shepherd for all" in whose heart is no evil and who seeks the stray flock, strikes at sin, and has the gods in his heart. The contrast here is oriented toward ethics. The "Prophecy of a Lamb" under King Bocchoris, once again presents the same contrast.[3] The glorious future is a change wrought by a victorious military expedition (invasion) against Syria. The "Prophecy of the Potter" under King Amenophis IV mentions calamities (the darkening of the sun) and a period of great lawlessness.[4] Then a king arises who will bring in a state of blessedness so great that many will wish that the dead may rise to partake of it.

There is some question about the reliability of these accounts or translations and the very existence of these ideas. Lange[5] first translated the texts[6] in 1903. Six years later, he and Gardiner[7] eliminated all eschatology from them.[8] Gardiner reduces the original documents to nothing more than a picture of bad times in contrast with a hope of better times and a deliverance by Re.[9] The first document concerns a contemporary king. The peculiar phrases are characteristic of Oriental court style. At the time of the king's installation, these predictions were uttered. His reign would be one of great prosperity or, if he acted wickedly, the opposite. We conclude that the documents present the contrast between calamity and blessedness as found here upon the earth. Thus, the prophecies do not speak of eschatological events properly so called, but of temporal reversals only. Supernatural considerations do not enter in. At best, we can perhaps say that the language does not prove eschatology as such, but simply tells us that there must have been a belief in a literal eschatology of some kind from which these terms were borrowed.

In Assyrio-Babylonian eschatology, Marduk, god of the Light and Sun, is also god of salvation and deliverance. New Year is celebrated with a feast of Marduk in which he is presented as the one who will introduce a new year, i.e., a new world order, into the people's lives. Some of their kings seem to have been deified; not only are they favored by a god, but they are even begotten of a god and sometimes called gods. This is so especially when they are born of an unknown father or born in secret, i.e., under these circumstances they lay claim to divine birth. Gudea (ca. 2200 B.C.)[10] calls himself a god begotten of the god (deis), Gatum-dug.[11] This is also the case with Sargon I,[12] Naram-Sin,[13] and Assurbanipal I (ca. 650 B.C.).[14] In all probability we have here an eschatological background. It has often been asserted that the Old Testament Scriptures do not speak of the Messiah as God. This pagan eschatology opens this assertion to grave doubt. The contrast between calamity and blessedness is also presented in these documents in association with the accession of the monarch (so-called courtier's speech). If his rule is good, the monarch is congratulated as the introducer of a period of bliss and vice-versa. In the latter case, the idea of a curse is emphasized, mention is made of the trouble between man and man, and the darkening of the sun and moon is projected. It should be noted that these factors are also biblical.

The concept of world-cycles is the notion that, by means of a succession of eras leading up to a point where the original point is reached anew, the process begins over again. Seneca quotes from a priest, Berosus (ca. 280 B.C.), who taught that the world would come to an end through great conflagration when there was an astral conjunction in the sign of Cancer; and that the world would be destroyed by a great inundation when there was an astral conjunction in the sign of Capricorn.[15] The view of the world-goal and historical-periodicity is also found here. By observing the "procession of the Sun," i.e., the forward movement of the sun-station at the time of the spring equinox in the Zodiac, they derived the idea of the return to the original station and thus the concept of a world-year. Most of this Babylonian eschatology comes from Berosus. He also offers a chronology of the pre-diluvian kings. They had 432,000 years (or, as is suggested, 12 months of 36,000 years) completing one world-cycle and ending with the deluge.[16] The post-diluvian world-years are speculated upon from the activity of the sun. It was noticed that the sun started at the sign of the twins (Gemini) and went clear around through all the signs of the Zodiac until it got back to the twins, thus completing a cosmical year (world-year). Through the completion of the cosmical year there was a return to pristine conditions.

We comment upon all this as follows. Observe that the changes contemplated in the "courtier's speech" are not absolute, but rather political and economic. On the other hand, the extravagant language seems to be eschatological in origin. The idea of a supernatural origin of certain kings may have eschatological background in some messianic belief. Finally, the astronomical observations imply a certain approach to eschatology (i.e., periodicity; the end corresponding to the beginning). Nevertheless, true eschatology is lacking because the endless recurrence of world-cycles presents no prospect of an endless state of blessedness as our view presents.

We turn now to Persian eschatology. It is not based upon a process of astronomical changes, but upon the conflict between two powers, good (Ahura-Mazda, Ohrmazd) and evil (Angra Mainyu, Ahriman). In other words, the conflict here moves to a definite (in part at least) goal of an ethical complexion. The issue is the final supremacy of the good power. The eschatological elements in Persian eschatology are as follows: the end of the ethical conflict resulting in judgment, resurrection, and the final supremacy of the good preliminary judgment after death; appearance of a number of saviors during the later stage of the process (at intervals); appearance of the Savior at the end; universalism of salvation, i.e., all men become blessed; periodicity in the process, i.e., six thousand years of quiet before the struggle between the two opposing powers followed by six thousand years of turmoil and destruction by fire; finally, the period of bliss.

This brings us much closer to the biblical view than the other eschatologies. There are here even parallels to New Testament messianic ideas. Yima was considered the first king of the golden age (a first Adam). Together with his subjects, he was transferred to a future life (paradise). It is said that this same idea of conjoining is found in the New Testament, e.g., Christ and believers, the wolf and the lamb, etc. It is also pointed out that in the Old Testament phrase "Son of Man" (i.e., a Hebrew idiom for a distinctive man), we find an allusion to this first man. It is therefore claimed that this eschatology affected biblical eschatology in terms of the Son of Man figure and the idea of paradise.

In criticism of the view of biblical dependence on Persian eschatology, observe that this elaborate scheme, as such, is not found in the Avesta, but only in later books. Thus, the antiquity of these books is uncertain. Some scholars place them so late that their dependence could well have been upon the Bible. The French scholar, Darmesteter, places them very late.[17] A fully developed scheme as found in the Bible is not found in the Avesta. The messianic elements are much later (perhaps about A.D. 200). The resemblance to biblical eschatology may be due to the semi-ethical and militant character of the Persian religion. It works in the direction of historicizing the events of the world, thus giving a progressive view and ultimately an eschatology. However, the difference must not be lost sight of. There is no redemptive element, properly speaking, in Persian eschatology. Ethical elements are mixed with physical, ritual conceptions (i.e., clean and unclean are imperfectly separated from the ethical elements). Much in the field of eschatology is accomplished by magical compulsion, even above the activities of the gods. The precise question under debate is the theory of some scholars (e.g., Bousset)[18] that the eschatological ideas in the intercanonical Jewish apocalypses are due to Persian influence via Babylonia. Some deny this.

The final example of pagan thought is the eschatological ideas in the Hellenistic period, i.e., Greece and Rome under the influence of syncretism. One of the chief characteristics of this variety is the peculiar use of the *Soter* title. The title is transferred from gods, demigods, and heroes first to human rulers after death, then to living rulers. The development of the use of this term in Greek history is as follows. First, it was used in ancient Greek religion for the gods and demigods. Then during the Hellenistic period after Alexander the Great, it was given to earthly rulers, but only after death and with great hesitation. Later it was used boldly by living kings, particularly by the Ptolemies of Egypt and the Seleucids of Assyria (Syria). Finally, the Roman magistrates adopted the term and applied it to themselves. Up to the time of Constantine, the emperor was called the savior of the human race. It was not meant only in a political sense, but also in a religious sense. The emperor was the head of the cult and expected to be worshiped; thus, a semi-deification. In Egypt, Augustus was called " the Son of the Sun," "Beloved of Ra and Isis," "the Lord of Lords." (This may be merely eschatological terminology rather than eschatology itself.) The distinctively eschatological elements (particularly in Roman eschatology) are a new world-period (*lustrum*); a period of world-blessedness headed up by new rulers.

This eschatology is found in the following sources. First, we see it in the Fourth Eclogue of Virgil (ca. 40 B.C.), where fantastic expectations are connected with the birth of a child of Pollio.[19] Virgil connects the event with the return of a golden age, i.e., the age of Saturn. The son will be a god and a wonder to the gods. He will bring peace to the world of politics and to the world of nature (i.e., among the animals). Before this, there will be a brief period of conflict, specifically, another Trojan War or Argonaut expedition. This period is described as one in which ships will no longer sail the seas, commerce will be unnecessary, the earth will produce everything, agriculture will not need to be practiced, and wool will grow dyed upon the sheep's back.

We comment that this conception presents a new *lustrum*, an era of sacrifice and cleansing. It has a biblical coloring (i.e., before bliss comes atonement). The Sibyl predicted that this was the last time; the world was entering a return to the original cycle, i.e., to the age of Saturn.[20] This view has cosmical elements. Virgil hoped to become the Homer of this period. Since he wrote after the strife between Octavius and Anthony (40 B.C.), it seems difficult to conclude that the poet believed all this of the son of Pollio. It is probably an imitation of the Oriental court style. Nevertheless, it is striking that the supernatural plays such a role here. This is beyond that of the Babylonians and may be due to poetic fancy to a large extent.

Second, in the Aeneid,[21] which was written about 23 B.C., Anchises prophesies to his son that Augustus will reign from sea to sea in the age of Saturn. Thus, what was written about the son of Pollio is here ascribed to Augustus.

Third, decrees and inscriptions of the Asiatic provinces related to the reign of Augustus stated that he would receive certain honors given to "the divine Savior of the world." His birthday was the beginning of a new order of things, for he had given a new face to the world ("world-renovator") and God gave him new power. In addition, his birthday marks "the beginning of a new gospel," and thus the calendar is changed. New year begins on September 23. This is extravagant language that is obviously not political, but eschatological.

How do we explain all of this? First, there is a natural eudaemonistic desire in the human heart to place a blessed state beyond the present. Perhaps this is due to a vague remembrance of the original state (of paradise). At any rate, there is nothing new in the Roman eschatology; the whole is a Hellenistic adaptation of Oriental (perhaps even Old Testament) ideas as described above. Second, it might also be traced as a remnant of ancient revelation before that revelation was limited to a special people. The Bible teaches that such a revelation, which is older than soteriology (pre-redemptive), did exist. Should it be any wonder that an idea of such antiquity should hold out? It receives, after the entrance of sin, a new form, but not outside Israel. The older remnants nevertheless may have remained in the world-people. Then again, it might be traced partially to the astronomical observations of the Babylonians. Finally, since Virgil wrote from 40 to 23 B.C., he might very well have been influenced by the Old Testament and other Jewish literature. However, this idea of dependence upon the Old Testament is highly debatable.

3

THE PRESENT JUNCTURE
IN THE HISTORY OF
OLD TESTAMENT ESCHATOLOGY

We begin with the different valuations placed upon the importance of the eschatological material in the Old Testament. A very high estimation is placed upon it by the conservative theology in order to uphold the continuity and identity between the Old and New Testaments. Eschatology was viewed as the backbone of Old Testament prophecy and religion because the Old Testament was studied chiefly as an explanation of the New Testament (new covenant). In addition, the interests of apologetics were served by the conservative view, i.e., the New Testament peoples were the subject of predictive prophecy. Finally, on account of the soteric importance of Old Testament eschatology, it was highly esteemed. Others, however, placed a very low estimation upon the subject. On account of its antisupernaturalistic subjectivizing tendency, eschatology was not congenial to the rationalistic mind. All supernatural and objective eschatological elements are discarded by this approach.

Let us consider the attitude of the Wellhausen school toward Old Testament eschatology as a form of acute rationalism. According to this approach, the religious history of Israel is interpreted in terms of its origin, development, and philosophy. The religious value of the Old Testament is found in its ethical monotheism. Emphasis upon eschatology threatens to detract from this and, moreover, to throw weight upon things inconsistent with eschatology. Therefore, according to Wellhausen, the eschatological element is not an essential element of the Old Testament. Rather, it was roped in at a comparatively later date due to a peculiar combination of events. This school attempts to place or reduce everything to one principle, and this results largely in undervaluing the Old Testament. There is no eschatology proper in the earlier (pre-prophetic) religion of Israel. The reason for this is that the religion is particularistic and has no wider outlook than the momentary destiny of Israel. Jehovah is not God of a world-process, but of one people. Therefore, the cosmic and universalistic elements cannot be very old in Old Testament eschatology. In other words, Jehovah as a national God could not have been regarded as the head of a true eschatology with cosmic elements. If there was any eschatology in the early period, it must have been primitive, i.e., a hope that Israel would come to great prosperity.

The physical elements, i.e., the changing relation between the beasts and the condition of the desert, are nonethical and cannot be traced to the prophets, who are purely ethical. They predicted only historical judgments. Thus, physical eschatology is due not to the prophets, but to later apocalyptic literature.

The ethical elements, and these alone, originated from the prophets of the eighth century B.C. on. Wellhausen himself thinks that the eschatology of woe preceded the eschatology of weal. The prophets in their time were nothing but prophets of woe, forecasting threats exclusively. Psychologically and historically, this was born from their protest against the sin of Israel coupled with the threat of foreign invasion and destruction of the state. As an afterthought, they created a foil, i.e., an eschatology of weal. This consisted of a patriotic attachment to Israel and led to a softening of the harshness of the prospect of woe by means of a hope of restoration beyond. These two prospects are believed conceivable in the same mind with slight chronological separation. This change, including the messianic idea as a part of the eschatology of weal, is to be found in one and the same prophet. The messianic idea arose as a protest against the present king and kingdom. It was a picture of an ideal kingdom. This fixes the date about the time of the breach between the prophets and the king (ca. 800 B.C.).

The extreme wing of this school holds that these thoughts could not have originated in the same mind. The eschatology of weal is centuries older and went directly against the prophetic ideal of exclusive woe. Thus, the addition of weal to woe is a much later occurrence (not later in the minds of the same prophets, but in the minds of the later prophets). In 1897, Paul Volz wrote as follows on the pre-exilic Jehovah prophecy and the Messiah in their mutual relation.[1] The messianic idea is foreign to the spirit of true pre-exilic prophecy, which preached nothing but judgment. There is no messianic prophecy before Ezekiel! In the writings of the prophets from Amos to Ezekiel, there is not a single passage proving the presence of the messianic idea. Messianic elements now found in the earlier prophets are due to later redaction (after Ezekiel). The messianic element in Ezekiel and after was not imbued by a genuine spirit of prophecy (which is ethical, remember), but by a spirit of prophetic decadence. This pattern is alleged to be observable in the following points.

Genuine prophecy is ethical; messianic prophecy is magically supernaturalistic. Every messianic idea stands for the bringing in of a new order of things by some miraculous power. The prophets, as ethical absolutists, were absorbed in the one idea of justice; hence they knew of no miraculous power. Genuine prophecy tends toward universalism; messianic prophecy, toward particularism and patriotism. The Messiah is a national-political figure for Israel whose purpose is to uphold internal order and lead in successful warfare. The prophets were completely divorced from this. Genuine prophecy is antiroyalistic; messianic prophecy makes the royal figure of the Messiah central. Genuine prophecy is ethical, pure and simple (concerned with justice);

messianic prophecy presents an idea of grace, i.e., undeserved bliss. The critics believe that the high idea of justice was the result of development and that there was, therefore, little danger of returning to the primitive idea of a God of grace. (Note: even according to the less radical, generally accepted Wellhausen scheme, messianic prophecy presupposes a break between the kings and the prophets.)

According to all (not merely the specific sense of Volz's view stated above), the influence of Ezekiel marks an epoch in the development of Old Testament eschatology. In the pre-Ezekiel source, prophecy was the result of minds working on historical experiences. The method was psychological and historical. It had well-defined limits and kept in touch with reality. Consequently, naturalism colored eschatology. The Ezekiel source of prophecy or eschatology is based on speculation and reflection. Prior to this, it was controlled by historical experiences, but now by literary inspiration. The creative element began to work and worked in new material. Some of the elements are these: the physical (nonethical) element is introduced into the prophetic forecast, culminating in the "new heaven and new earth" of the later Isaiah; the horizon widens, becoming physically and internationally cosmical; the ethical element recedes into the background; there is an influx of foreign, Oriental material.

How does the critical school account for this? It is connected with their theological position. Wellhausen values the Old Testament and the prophets because of and in proportion to their ethical spirit. The value of Israelite religion lies in its ethical monotheism. But the religion of Israel is the soteric religion par excellence. Eschatology is closely connected with the soteric element. Eschatology is the matrix of the whole conception of salvation. Now, the ethical and soteric elements are not irreconcilable. With the critics, ethics has overgrown true religion and ousted eschatology. We reply that the redemptive idea is central. Eschatology is the matrix of the entire concept of salvation.

The reaction from the Wellhausen school has proceeded under the influence of Assyrio-Babylonian studies—the school of

Gunkel and Gressmann. These modern Oriental scholars strike a severe blow at Wellhausen. This is especially true of Gunkel in his *Creation and Chaos*[2] (Harnack scornfully designated the contents of the book by its title)[3] and Gressmann in *The Origin of Israelite and Jewish Eschatology*.[4] Both believe in an intensive Babylonian influence in early Israel. Since the Babylonians had great influence over the Israelites, these eschatological elements must have been injected into the Israelite religion. Gunkel and Gressmann employed the same method that Wellhausen used and opposed him only in the matter of philosophical construction. They, too, believed that the law was older than the prophets. They got this knowledge by reading between the lines of the prophets and discovering the presuppositions of the writers. Wellhausen never applied this method in trying to find eschatology in Israelite religion, simply because he looked upon eschatology as a product of the prophets. These Babylonian investigators, on the other hand, believed that there was eschatology in ancient Israel. They found it there by employing the Wellhausen method of reading between the lines. Gunkel and Gressmann had a grievance against the Wellhausen school, i.e., that it emphasized too much the when rather than the whence of the origin of these books. Wellhausen has made literary development identical with actual development. Gunkel and Gressmann say that a thing existed long before it makes its appearance in record. According to them, there must have been eschatology in Israel's religion from the earliest (pre-prophetic times).

Elements in the Gunkel–Gressmann scheme are as follows: exegetical findings are used to point out the presence of ancient eschatological material in Israelite religion; the importation of this element from Babylonia is hypothesized; to the popular use of this material is ascribed a nonethical (purely mythological) form and belief that it was first ethicized by the prophets. We comment that these three were not originally connected. Thus, one may agree with the results of the one and not of the other. Wellhausen says that eschatology was not there; Gunkel says that it was there and that it came from Babylon. We say that it was partially due to revelation.

The exegetical induction of the Gunkel–Gressmann view has found a pre-prophetic eschatology. Before Amos, the populace had an eschatology and connected it with divine worship. This is inferred from the manner in which the prophets took for granted the people's acquaintance with an eschatology. Amos speaks of the "day of judgment" not as something of which they have the wrong conception ("woe unto you that desire the day of the Lord," Amos 5:18). They found a two-sided eschatology in the Old Testament consisting of a dread of woe and a hope of weal. Amos 5:18 suggests that the people were hopeful about the coming of Jehovah. The dark element, we find in Amos 6:3 ("you put far away the day of Jehovah"). Some think that Israel considers it dark only for other nations. However, Amos 6:3 and Isaiah 5:19ff. suggest that there was a party recognizing it as a day of evil. It is true that some thought it very near and that it would pass them by, but both elements are there. They found nature-elements inherent in the prophetic as well as the popular eschatology, although with a difference of emphasis. The prophets tell us that not only will the solution of the crisis take place by a historical, political force, but also by a natural upheaval. The beginnings of the cosmic-universalistic aspect is traceable in the early pre-prophetic eschatology. In Wellhausen's view (with respect to the physical element), the idea of eschatology originated with the prophets when they became conscious of a probable Assyrian invasion and connected that with judgment. The physical element entered later when the prophets degenerated. They enlarged the idea and gave it a cosmical aspect. This was not prior to the Deutero-Isaiah period.

We suggest the following objections to the critical view. Gunkel and Gressmann underethicize the popular eschatology (weal), while hyperethicizing the prophetic eschatology (woe). They say that from the beginning in the ancient documents, wherever Jehovah is encountered, great natural upheavals are mentioned. Nature belongs to the eschatological field of action.

Amos (1:14; 2:2; 6:8; 8:9) mentions in this connection: war, earthquake, pestilence, solar eclipse, etc. War here does not appear as a matrix of eschatology, but simply as a coordinate element. Amos hardly mentions the Assyrians. It is therefore a gross exaggeration to make this element so prominent in prophetic eschatology. Hosea (4:3; 13:14–15) speaks of death, Sheol, and the east wind. In Hosea, we find the nature-forces most prominent. As to war, he places Assyria on a par with Egypt and war is looked upon as no more than a coordinate element. Isaiah (2:12–19; 24:4; 33:9; 34:4) speaks of the elements in eschatology in the same way. The great eschatological passages in chapters 2 and 9 do not mention Assyria. In 7:18, Assyria is placed on a par with Egypt.

The various eschatological elements seem to have been coordinate as far as the time of their origin is concerned. And if there is any distinction to be made in the order of these elements, it would be as follows: calamity, war, Assyria. In pre-prophetic times this element of natural upheaval can be found among the populace in the same way that any eschatology can be traced to the people. This knowledge is assumed on the part of the people by the prophets. It is very illogical for Wellhausen to pronounce these elements a creation of the prophets because Palestine itself was not subject to these natural upheavals. Therefore, this material could hardly be Palestinian and, if it is a derived element, it must be older and it must have its source outside Palestine. The content of these physical elements shows that it is usually drawn from theophanies. Much of this material is, however, foreign to Palestine. Earthquakes, tempests (especially the southeast wind), and floods were distinctly Palestinian. Volcanic eruptions are not to be found in Palestine, yet they are repeatedly referred to (cf. Nah. 1:6; Mic. 1:3–4, 6 ; Mal. 3:19; Deut. 32:22; Ps. 97:5). Then, too, these elements are found in the prophets unharmonized. If this material were invented, we would expect to find an attempted unification. In Amos, we find famine, fire, war, and calamity placed side by side without any attempt at harmonization. Then, too, the nature imagery is sometimes changed to military invasion, e.g., the flood in Isaiah 28:1ff. is changed into an Assyrian invasion. The original idea was that of a flood, and to that was added the idea of political development. The original idea, however, is still maintained.

We may summarize the arguments for the pre-prophetic aspect of the physical elements in Israelite eschatology. First, some elements are foreign to Canaan and must have been present to them before the entrance into Canaan. Second, there is an absence of a harmonizing attempt with respect to the different elements. Third, there is a development in applying the physical elements to political phenomena.

The Gunkel–Gressmann school found a universalistic element inherent in the ancient eschatology. This universalistic view is found in respect to both the eschatology of woe and that of weal in Isaiah and Micah, but the critics declare these references to be late. However, this is also found in Zephaniah 2:4, 12; 3:10, where Gaza, Ashkelon, Ethiopia, etc. are included in the eschatological outlook. (Note: Zephaniah is considered sound, even by the critics.) The critics offer two explanations for this universalistic element. First, the rise of Assyria initiated this idea. Assyria was their enemy and therefore it is included among the judged. But no mention is made of the sin of these foreign peoples, and that is what we would expect if Zephaniah had introduced them into the scope of eschatology. The above suggestion demands an ethical background also in respect to foreigners. The introduction of fish and birds shows that it is connected with the general idea of matter, and one would hardly expect that the animal kingdom would be affected merely inside Palestine. Second, it is a homiletical device to impress the people with the uselessness of resistance. In criticism, it is not the Assyrians, but Jehovah, who will destroy the nations. If the natural element is old, it could not have been limited to Israel. Isaiah 64:1–3 and Micah 1:3–4 say that Jehovah will shake the earth, not the land. The idea of the return of Paradise is not local. Hosea 2:18 predicts that battle will be ousted from the land. Now this could not have been local because he is describing a condition of absolute safety. If we take it as local, then Israel would be without defense and therefore by no means safe. The physical element is interwoven with the universal element. Therefore, if the idea of the return of paradise is old, then this universalistic element must be old.

The Gunkel–Gressmann school also found a messianic element in the ancient eschatology. According to the critical view, the messianic element is placed late by Wellhausen and even some more conservative men because: (1) it presupposes a historic kingdom; and (2) it presupposes the breach between the kings and the prophets. By way of refutation, we note that aside from an earthly kingship, the prophets had a conception of a Jehovah-kingship. Jehovah was essentially king in his relation to Israel. Then, too, the following elements can be found: (a) a nonroyal figure of the Messiah; (b) a royal Messiah not connected with David; (c) a royal Messiah dynastically connected with David. These findings are evident first in Micah (ca. 800 B.C.), who speaks of a coming ruler whose going forth is from eternity and whose mother travails (Mic. 5:2–4). This idea is connected with the Davidic line. Micah speaks of these terms as quite common and assumes the people's acquaintance with them. Second, Isaiah 11:1, 10 mentions the house of David. Isaiah 9:6 says a child is born unto us (this is spoken of as well-known material). It is too abrupt to be new. Isaiah 7:14 mentions a young woman as something well-known. Third, Amos and Hosea do not speak of the king, but restrict themselves to the restoration of the kingdom. Fourth, Psalm 45 speaks in extraordinary terms of a living king. Critics claim that this is but eschatological language used at the accession of a king, but then the eschatological must have been older. The old view considers this passage as a representation of a king typical of the Messiah. Finally, Genesis 49 and Numbers 24 present the Shiloh prophecy and the Balaam oracles. (There is a modern tendency to rehabilitate these prophecies; they were once rejected.) These are again looked upon as messianic. The Shiloh

71

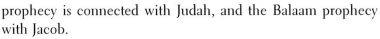

prophecy is connected with Judah, and the Balaam prophecy with Jacob.

Summary of the findings of Gunkel and Gressmann:

a. a pre-prophetic eschatology;
b. a physical element in the earliest prophecy;
c. a two-sided eschatology;
d. a universalistic eschatology;
e. a messianic eschatology.

Criticism: Gressmann differs from us as to the origin of this material. He says that it is Babylonian; we say that it is common Israelite tradition based upon revelation. Insofar as it has material common to that of the Babylonian, it may have been Babylonian. Gressmann holds that the popular eschatology had a mythological origin and was of that character, while the prophets, being dominated by ethical motives, had an ethical eschatology. This stems from these facts: (1) He overemphasizes the prophets' ethical tendency. For when he says that the ethical element was the main one, he is off because the prophets had an interest in the physical elements, which was not confined to homiletical adaptability and which showed the relation of natural corruption and sin (i.e., the ethical element). Nature is used to bring out the transcendent greatness and majesty of Jehovah. (2) He underemphasizes popular beliefs. In answer to this, notice that the ethical element was not wanting among the people. God's infliction of a calamity is called a "visitation," which has an ethical coloring. In ancient representation, God is judge as well as king; thus, this includes an ethical idea. The technical term for victories is righteousness, which shows an appreciation of a victory from an ethical viewpoint.

4

ESCHATOLOGY IN ITS
PRE-REDEMPTIVE STAGE

It is not biblical to hold that eschatology is a sort of appendix to soteriology, a consummation of the saving work of God. Eschatology is not necessarily bound up with soteriology. So conceived, it does not take into account that a whole chapter of eschatology is written before sin. Thus, it is not merely an omission to ignore the pre-redemptive eschatology; it is to place the sequel in the wrong place. There is an absolute end posited for the universe before and apart from sin. The universe, as created, was only a beginning, the meaning of which was not perpetuation, but attainment. The principle of God's relation to the world from the outset was a principle of action or eventuation. The goal was not comparative (i.e., evolution); it was superlative (i.e., the final goal).

This goal was not only previous to sin, but irrespective of sin. For the sake of plainness, let us distinguish between the goal as an absolute, perfect, ethical relation to God and as a supernaturalizing of man and the world. These elements are intimately related, but logically distinct. Both of these elements could have been realized apart from sin and redemption. The ethical element could have been carried to the highest point of unchangeable rectitude. Similarly, the supernaturalizing element could

73

have been realized apart from sin. The relation of these two is also conceivable on the same basis, i.e., apart from sin. In sum, the original goal remains regulative for the redemptive development of eschatology by aiming to rectify the results of sin (remedial) and uphold, in connection with this, the realization of the original goal as that which transcends the state of rectitude (i.e., rising beyond the possibility of death in life eternal). The nonredemptive strand explains the preeminence of the natural (physical) element in biblical eschatology. Thus, it is not a mere question of the conversion of man (absolute ethical relation to God), but of the transformation and supernaturalizing of the world.

To this original eschatology is now added a soteric force. It retained its original purpose, but now has a soteric form. The end that it deals with is the end of a saving process. The two great acts of the eschatological drama (i.e., resurrection and judgment) plainly have a remedial significance. Nevertheless, there was something in the pre-redemptive eschatology that was not eliminated but reincorporated in the redemptive program. Eschatology aims at consummation rather than restoration. Therefore, redemptive eschatology must be restorative and consummative. It does not aim at the original state, but at a transcendental state of man. It must be curative and tonic. Every act of salvation must be medical and supernaturalizing whereby man is not made merely normal, but is prepared for the supernormal. It is at this point that we find the great difference between soteriology and eschatology. It is a goal unreachable by the pure spiritual element. The supernaturalizing aspect suggests this thought, for the goal demands radical change in the physical and spiritual. It does not mean that the people had departed from the right idea (as Gunkel and Gressmann maintain) and that these expressions were but a manner of expression in mythological terms. There was no conflict in the mind of the prophets. The nature-elements are not antireligious. The prophets were biblical in holding that the absolute goal could not be attained without the nature-elements. They had a purer religious and eschatological instinct.

This eschatological destiny may be verified from an examination of Genesis 1–3. The phrase *the final state* equals *paradise* (i.e., its return). This "return of paradise" does not point to a higher state, however. It proves no more than that the redemptive program includes a restoration of the normal state. The tree of life contains a prophetic element (cf. Gen. 3:22). The narrative plainly excludes the idea that man was without life—religious, physical, and ethical. The distinction is between a life in possession and one in prospect. It is eternal life in prospect. The essence of eschatology lies in this prospective element. The seventh day, i.e., the *Sabbath*, may also be viewed as an eschatological term. The Sabbath finds its prototype in the life and works of God. Thus, it means fulfillment; not cessation and weariness, but consummation. This rest of consummation was introduced into the life of man in order to show him his goal. Even in unfallen man the Sabbath was an eschatological sign because its meaning lies in the relation of man and God. It is important to note this because it bears witness to the fundamental element of eschatology in religion. Eschatology is the essence of true religion as is shown by its pre-redemptive existence.

Two principles stand out in this primeval eschatology. First, the intimate conjunction between eschatology and ethics. We have here the possibility of an attainment of a higher state, but it is conditioned by obedience. The way of the tree of life is the tree of knowledge. The tree of life, although a sacrament, does not give life magically. The ethical character of the future life is symbolized by the ethical approach. Second, as to its content, it is highly religious. Highest life is characterized by the most intimate connection with God. Paradise is spoken of as a garden of God (cf. Isa. 51:3; Gen. 3:8). The land of the gods in Greek mythology expresses an idea similar to this. The tree of life is in the center of the garden of God. Sometimes mention is made of the streams of God or the streams of life. This is brought in close connection with the deity because they flow from the mountain of God (cf. Pss. 36:8ff.; 46:4ff.; Joel 3:18; Ezek. 47:1–7). The future paradise is spoken of as the paradise of God (cf. Rev. 2:7). The eschatological state is a theocentric state. All false eudaemonism, from which unbiblical speculation opens a wider door, finds a barrier here. The physical element is subservient to the ethical and religious.

5

ESCHATOLOGY IN THE FIRST
REDEMPTIVE REVELATION

Eschatology is older than soteriology because it is precisely in the redemptive revelation immediately following that little is said of eschatology. The divine method was to impress the religious and moral aspects of sin. Therefore, sinful man was not to be soothed and to make light of his fault and to be comforted by a promise of a greater state. Theological speculation that stresses eschatology in this connection forgets the redemptive plus. As it was natural before sin to point to eschatology, so it is natural to point to redemption now. There is an expulsion from paradise, but not one word of a better paradise. The destiny of man is tied down to the lower world. Victory over the seed of the serpent is promised. Although this does point to a final issue, it does not look beyond a restoration. The complexion would be more eschatological if we could interpret the seed of the woman as the Messiah. But the following objections oppose this.

First, the seed of the woman and the seed of the serpent are parallel. The seed of the serpent must be interpreted collectively because it is distinct from the serpent itself. Therefore, seed of the woman must also be taken collectively. Second, the seed of the woman points to a human source, while Messiah is always spoken of as divine and of a divine source. Third, the Holy Spirit gives the expression a collective interpretation in Romans 16:20. Fourth, it must be admitted that the form allows a messianic inference. The two forces at issue are the serpent and the seed of the woman. That it is put in this way must be of significance. The power of evil is concentrated in the serpent, and therefore we would expect a similar concentration in the seed of the woman. Indirectly, then, there is a suggestion of a messianic idea in the concentration "seed of the Serpent" in the one serpent at the final issue. Fifth, this raises the whole question of whether the collective representation of the eschatological process is more ancient in the Old Testament than the individualized "messianic" one. If the promise of the "seed of the woman" is understood in a personal sense, then the so-called messianic form of the prophecy would be older. But even then, this claim could not be made in an unqualified manner because the collective purport of the word *seed* is also there under all circumstances. Thus, the "seed of the woman" has for its opposite the "seed of the serpent," which must be collective.

The only question under debate concerns this: whether assuming that both elements are present, the main stress rests on the collective idea or on the personalized form of it. We incline to believe that the former is the case. In other words, this is a prediction that out of the circle of the human race, here called "the seed of the woman," the fatal blow will be struck that bruises the serpent's head and so brings things to a final issue. On the other view, it would have been easy to formulate the clause differently so as to remove all ambiguity through stating that the "child of the woman" was to bruise the head of the serpent. As it is, we have the personal serpent and the nonpersonalized "seed of the woman."

On the other hand, there is no truth in the theory that the concept of the Messiah is a late importation into the Old Testament world of eschatological ideas. There is only this much truth in this, i.e., that the name *Messiah* is of comparatively late appearance. It does not occur until the Psalms. The reason for this is that "the Messiah" was not meant to become the name of the eschatological mediator until the expectation of an eschatological mediator by the side of God had become linked with the promise made to the house of David. He could not be called "the Anointed of Jehovah" until Jehovah had caused David and his successors to be anointed. But his figure was familiar long before, whatever names may have been given to him. Although the protevangelium may have to be interpreted collectively, it appears from the words of Lamech (Gen. 5:29), the father of Noah, spoken at the birth of his son that the belief and expectation were prevalent at the time that somebody in the line of patriarchal descent would be born who would be hailed as the great Restorer of the normal conditions of human life which, as they were at that time, were recognized as abnormal and crying out for deliverance ("this same shall comfort us concerning our work and toil of our hands [which arise from] the ground which Jehovah has cursed"). This derives evil, economic, and agricultural conditions directly from the curse and indirectly from sin because it had been in the curse pronounced after the primordial sin of man that this evil accursed condition had been decreed for the soil.

You will notice that while this decollectivizes the first promise, nevertheless it does not go so far as to attach the personalized form of the expectation to any particular section of the race. Noah no more than his father, Lamech, seems to have had any historical perspective about the matter. The father thought that his child might be the instrument of fulfillment. If Noah did not cherish such short-sighted expectations after him, it may have been due to the fact that the religious and moral condition of his children did not invite such hopefulness or encourage it.

6

THE ESCHATOLOGICAL
BACKGROUND OF THE DELUGE

The cosmical extent of the deluge-event is both negative and positive. First, negatively, the flood destroyed the world (cf. Gen. 6). This is a catastrophic world-judgment. This fact is confirmed by pagan mythology, where it is associated with the chaos-flood out of which the world arose. The creation and the deluge both have cosmic significance. It was not confined to man; but the purpose was that God repented that he had created the world. Second, positively, it is the commencement of a new world-order. The waters receded on the first day of the month and the first month of the year (cf. Gen. 8:13); therefore, a new year. It also possibly attaches itself to the periodicity of history and the *berith*-principle. Periodicity is generally shown by the covenants that appear at the beginnings of periods. Now the deluge and the post-diluvian order of things prefigure eschatological crisis and the eschatological state. In other words, the deluge and "new creation" are typical of the absolute end of the world and the final renewal of the world.

This is confirmed by the fact that Genesis 8:22 promises that the catastrophe will not be repeated "while the earth remaineth." The catastrophe will not be repeated before the end of the world. This promise protects against a return of the catastrophe that would disturb the processes of nature, while allowing for a catastrophe that will change the processes of nature (thus a termination in the end of the world).

Then, too, the imagery of the flood is used for eschatological description in prophecy and the Psalter. The Psalms and the prophets speak of an interposition of Jehovah in terms derived from the flood. These are either derived from the deluge or invented by the prophets. At all events, the connection between the deluge and what comes again is clear. In Psalm 29:10, Jehovah sat as King; Jehovah will sit as King. Isaiah pictures it militarily, but also as a direct interposition of God (cf. 17:12; 28:2, 15). Jeremiah 47:2 says the water will overflow from the north. This is not natural, because there is little chance of a flood from the north. In Isaiah 24:18, the destruction is caused by opening the windows of heaven (cp. Isa. 54:9, "this is as the waters of Noah unto thee"). In the new covenant with Israel the Noahian pledge is reenacted on a higher stage (i.e., it is an eschatological pledge). Also, it is probable that the prophetic concept of the "remnant" is derived from the narrative of the deluge. This idea is older than the prophets because it existed in the expectation of the people.

Finally, the New Testament places the epoch of Noah in parallel with the second coming of Christ (cf. Matt. 24:37; Luke 17:26). These passages point out a comparison between the sinfulness immediately preceding the two periods under consideration. But it is especially the suddenness of the coming of Christ that is stressed in this connection. First Peter 3:20ff. compares the water of baptism with that of the flood. Both have an eschatological significance and are directed toward salvation. The water was an instrument of the world-judgment and separated godly and ungodly as it does in baptism. Hence, the "interrogation [*eperoteria*] of a good conscience" (v. 21) points ahead to the judgment. "Ye are sealed until the day of redemption," says Paul (Eph. 4:30). "Few are saved" points to the Old Testament idea of the remnant (1 Peter 3:20). Second Peter 3:5ff. presents a parallelism between the diluvian and final catastrophes. The present universe is preserved for fire. In this passage Peter controverts an anti-eschatological idea of the continuance of the present world. He speaks of the world that was and that now is. It is the Word of God that kept the ante-diluvian world compact and the Word is doing it now. The epistle of Clement points out that the deluge had eschatological significance in that Moses preached a regeneration of the world (cf. 1 Clement 9:4 with Matt. 19:28).

7

THE ESCHATOLOGICAL ELEMENT
IN THE THEOPHANIES

Redemptive eschatology is more than revelation. The typical signification of the deluge lies on the judgment side and not primarily on the side of redemption. The eschatology of nature is typical of the eschatology of redemption. Revelation in the patriarchal history foreshadows eschatology along the line of redemption. The expression "fire and brimstone" (Gen. 19:24) in connection with the destruction of the cities of the plain is expressive of the eschatology of judgment. This, however, is probably the chief, if not the only exception. But the main emphasis is on the redemptive side. Theophanies are personal representations of God in visible form. They go beyond the mere purpose of revelation; they express, in primitive form, God's approach to and communion with man. God does not merely speak in a theophany; he acts!

With respect to the past, the theophany represents the renewed approach from the past severance of God and man. This loss of fellowship was expressed in man's expulsion from paradise. The theophany marks the first step toward the return of the primitive, normal intercourse. With respect to the future, the theophany presents the renewal of the paradise-condition and as such presages a full future paradise. It points to the new world.

This significance is expressed in the locality of the theophanies. Notice that this form of self-disclosure is not expressed before the entrance into Canaan. It links theophanies with subsequent appearances of God in Canaan. These are but the beginning, and they differ from the later forms in their being momentary. They are simply visits. An approach toward permanent nearness is made by the building of altars, which are revisited as places that God might frequent. All this prepares for the permanent divine in-dwelling. Canaan prefigures the eschatological state of Israel. It is the land flowing with milk and honey; i.e., typical of paradise. Note that Canaan was afterwards the scene of the highest permanent theophany of the Old Testament (i.e., the temple) and therefore typical of the final consummate state of the theocracy.

The Angel of Jehovah stands for the completeness and comprehensibility of Jehovah. Through this Angel the theophany is limited to redemption; for the visibility of appearance belongs to redemption. This procedure of linking Jehovah with one figure is practically equivalent to the later Messiah. The significance of the Messiah is to make God's work and significance concrete. Thus, the *malach*-theophanies are real prophecies of the incarnation. The substantial reason is that the Messiah carries this principle to its logical conclusion, viz., that God is with us, Immanuel. Everything messianic is, in the last analysis, eschatological.

Theophanies become determinators of subsequent eschatological terminology. "Coming" or "advent" is the main eschatological term. "God comes" expresses the keynote of all eschatology. This is because the presence of God is of great eschatological concern. Hence, the importance of the parousia. In later times, the idea became more general. Even in patriarchal times, the term *coming* has reference to general eschatology and messianic eschatology. The epiphany of Christ and the parousia are ideas that ultimately come from the Old Testament.

Consider, finally, the condescending, friendly character of the theophany. This is more pronounced in the patriarchal period than later because "saving" was then emphasized in distinction from the "judging" later on. The supernatural is benevolent in its intent. Later imagery of eschatological language is largely theophanic. Jehovah comes in fire, earthquake, etc. These are absent from the patriarchal theophanies. It was natural that the saving element should be emphasized first because the center of eschatology is, in the first place, the saving and not the destruction of enemies.

8

THE SHILOH PROPHECY

The blessing pronounced by the patriarch Jacob upon his son, Judah, occupies quite a unique place among the blessings pronounced upon the tribes in general (cf. Gen. 49:10). This is the famous "Shiloh" prophecy. Numerous and large books have been written on it, and it cannot yet be said that the difficulties of interpretation are entirely cleared up. One great gain is to be registered. It has become increasingly clear, even among unbelieving scholars whose own religiosity is entirely weaned from every sort of messianic interest, that the clause referring to "Shiloh" is a mysterious messianic clause. The words of Jacob are: "The sceptre shall not depart from Judah, nor the judge's staff from between his feet, until Shiloh come, and unto him shall the obedience of the nations be."

Its incidental character is clear in that this is the only messianic reference in the patriarchal history. It presupposes a knowledge of messianic eschatology on the part of the people, for: (1) it is mentioned as well-known material; and (2) it is not introduced for its own purpose, but to express the permanence of Jehovah's rule (it will never "depart"). If it was an unknown term, it could not have been explanatory. The expression "until Shiloh comes" substantiates the idea of permanence. And this is made even stronger in some versions which have here "his

Shiloh." The idea is that Judah shall retain its rule forever, both pre-messianically and messianically. Since it is incidental, it is all the more important for us. If it had been introduced for its own sake, we could have made no inference. However, we are quite safe in assuming that it is older than prophecy. First, this follows from our view that it originated with Jacob; thus, the idea of Shiloh would be older than Jacob. Second, even on the critical ground that the idea was introduced after the death of Solomon (when the kingdom of David was rising), we can hold that it is older than David. Thus, we answer Wellhausen's assertion that it was introduced after the beginning of the decadence of the empire with which the messianic idea originated.

The periods in the history of the exegesis of "Shiloh" are as follows. The messianic interpretation, although erstwhile scoffed at, is now well assured. This is accepted independent of Shiloh itself. What Shiloh itself is, is still doubtful. This new conviction of the messianic interpretation of this prophecy is a return to ancient and medieval exegesis. The idea that Shiloh was a place (town) started in the eighteenth century as a revolt against the medieval interpretation. This was the fashionable interpretation on into the nineteenth century. The school of Hengstenberg was the only exception.[1] Dillmann[2] and Delitzsch,[3] who were comparatively orthodox theologians, accepted the nonmessianic idea. The stigma of unscholarliness was attached to the messianic Shiloh idea. Almost every scientific school now accepts the messianic idea. This should teach us the vanity of calling an idea antiquated.

The modern rehabilitation of the messianic interpretation is as follows. It began with the Wellhausen school. Wellhausen pointed out that it is absurd to look upon Shiloh here as a little town. The context and import of the passage show that Shiloh is a great universal thing. He proceeds on the assumption of the late origin of messianic prophecy and the dating of the "Blessing of Jacob" from the period of David–Solomon; thus, the messianically interpreted clause is a later interpolation. The school of Gunkel[4] and Gressmann[5] proceeded with the rehabilitation.

But they differ from Wellhausen in that they do not look upon this passage as an interpolation. They make the passage as old as the blessing is; the idea and the clause can easily be as old as David–Solomon—the two belong together. However, they do not place it as far back as we do.

The dissection of this prophecy and the arguments advanced in each case are as follows. The messianic idea is a product of the prophets. It arose when the state of affairs was so deplorable that a Messiah began to be looked upon as an only hope. We object to this on the grounds that the presumption is unwarranted. It is true that the messianic idea was revived about this time and that was probably due to the condition of affairs; i.e., the Messiah idea could have arisen from this Shiloh prophecy. This work of deliverance and restoration is Messiah's work, but he also had other functions; viz., ruler of nations, procurer of peace and blessedness as was typified in the Davidic and Solomonic reigns. The point is that the fact that deliverance was necessary could not account for the messianic idea.

This prophecy breaks the connection between verse 10a and verse 11 (so Wellhausen). These verses deal with the present condition of Judah and in between comes the Shiloh prophecy. It may be objected to this that Shiloh is not introduced for its own sake, but to affirm something about the reign of Judah mentioned in verse 10a. Besides, it may be questioned whether verse 11 refers to Judah; it may describe the messianic era.

The following context is too realistic and unspiritual to be mentioned in the same breath with the description of the Messiah. We counter that this objection shows a lack of historical and poetic sense on the part of the objectors. This passage dates back to the time when the people took a naive delight in physical blessedness. Even in the descriptions of the messianic era, the physical pictures are very pronounced. Physical delight and natural prosperity are mentioned as some of the factors of the new era. Note the following counter-considerations: (1) verse 10a requires something to complete it (this is suggested by the contents of the text itself); (2) the transition from 10a to 11 is very harsh, i.e., from glorification of Judah to a description of his wading in wine and milk.

The nonmessianic exegeses of this passage are as follows. First, Shiloh is a common noun meaning rest; thus, "until rest comes" or "until he comes to rest." This "rest" refers to the politically settled condition in Solomon's time; or it refers to the eschatological period (the latter cannot be regarded as really messianic). We object that Shiloh is not the usual word for "rest" in the Old Testament. *Shalal-Shala'-Shalam-Menuha'* occur in the sense of "rest." The root *shlh* means primarily "rest," but that word occurs only in Jeremiah 12:1 and Psalm 122:6. A noun of this root occurs nowhere. If it were a noun, we would expect Shilon; for *-on* is the ending of a common noun (which *-on* is sometimes, in proper nouns, changed to *-oo*). But the argument is that it is here simply a common noun (cp. Shelomom = Shelomoh).

Second, Shiloh is a proper noun and the name of a town in Ephraim where the tabernacle stood. There are two forms of this view. First, there is the rendering "as long as they [i.e., the people] come to Shiloh"; i.e., "forever." The idea here is that the sanctuary at Shiloh could never be destroyed (cf. Jer. 7:12, 14). The second view renders until "he" or "they" come to Shiloh; i.e., to set up the tabernacle there. The former rendering makes good sense; for it would mean that for a long time Judah would have the predominance. Consider the following objections: (1) the introductory phrase *ad ki* can never mean "as long as"; (2) the presupposition involved is that Shiloh existed from a time when she had the prospect of being an eternal sanctuary; i.e., from the time of the judges when the ark appeared in Shiloh. In Jacob's time the shrine at Shiloh was not such a popular shrine thought to be indestructible, if it existed at all! Either Jacob had first to foresee it and then form this manner of speaking on the basis of his foresight; or the prophecy was uttered after the setting up of the tabernacle at Shiloh and before David's time; but this suits neither the critical nor the orthodox view. Jeremiah (7:12ff.) states that the place was once reputed to be indestructible, but he goes on to ridicule the idea. It is absurd to hold that Jacob could formulate such a prophecy based upon an erroneous idea that the people would do so in the future; (3) Shiloh is unimportant on this view. Yet, the prophecy requires something of real importance for Shiloh; but, as a matter of fact on the critical assessment, it never was of cardinal importance. Joshua 18:1 presents it as a turning point in the history of Israel; i.e., between the period of conquest and possession. Judah did not lead people to Shiloh, nor did Judah come to Shiloh (for this reason, some render "until they come to Shiloh"); (4) it does not fit in with the idea of the passage on the critical view. The idea would be "Judah shall hold the scepter until he comes and ever afterwards." But there is no evidence that Judah ever possessed or retained the rule before or after it came to Shiloh. There must certainly be some connection between this passage and the rule of nations; otherwise this passage (prophecy) stands as a weak appendix, and the syntax is extremely weak; (5) looking at it retrospectively, there is nothing in history to which this idea might be applied (cf. Num. 2:2; 10:14; Judg. 1:2; 20:18). Scepter and ruler's staff are very specific, and Judah never possessed such a rule. Even the leadership before Shiloh was with Moses and Joshua.

Third, Delitzsch's modification of the town-Shiloh view gives a typical form.[6] According to him, there are three stages in the fulfillment of the prophecy. The placing of the tabernacle in Shiloh was a sign of the victory over the Canaanites with attendant peace afterwards. Thus, in the career of Judah the stages of war and peace were reenacted: first, as already mentioned, in the conquest of Canaan which was followed by peace after the setting up of the tabernacle at Shiloh; second, the warlike sway of David followed by the peaceful reign of Solomon—the erection of the temple; finally, the 'war' in the humiliation and passion of Christ followed by his exalted state of victory in heaven—his entrance into the heavenly tabernacle.

We list the following objections to this. (1) The structure of prophecy is not founded upon the principle of a contrast between war and peace. (2) The coming to Shiloh, while it might mark the beginning of more peaceful conditions, had nothing to do with the continuance of Judah's leadership, if such had existed. (3) The coming to Shiloh had nothing to do with the perpetuation of the rule of Judah. The building of the temple may have been and was in a certain sense instrumental in the perpetuation of David's reign. (4) The coming to Shiloh and the accession of Solomon did not precede, but followed the subjugation of the nations; in the text, it follows the introduction of the *shlh*-factor. The subjugation of the nations took place before the coming to Shiloh and not after as this prophecy (as Delitzsch views it) suggests. The coming to Shiloh and the building of the temple are not vitally connected with the subjugation of the nations. (5) Delitzsch looks upon this as if its fundamental construction was contrastic between war and peace, but it is really climactic; i.e., Judah will rule until something happens that will perpetuate this rule. The contrast that Delitzsch finds may be found in this passage in the figure of the lion: "Judah is a lion's whelp; from the prey, my son, thou art gone up: he stooped down, he couched as a lion and as a lioness who shall rouse him up" (Gen. 49:9). Then follows the Shiloh prophecy.

The messianic exegeses in their various forms are as follows. The oldest view is the most acceptable one. This view is based on reading *sheloh*, instead of *shiloh*, and rendering the passage "until he comes to whom it belongs" (*he asher lo*). The considerations favoring this view include the following. First is the omission of the *yodh*, which occurs in the oldest and the majority of manuscripts and documents.[7] The Codex Alexandrinus and Vaticanus read *heos an elthe ta apokeimena auto*, "until there come the things laid up for him"—messianic rule. The other texts read *heos an elthe ho apokeita*, "until he comes for whom it has been laid up"—the messianic ruler. The question of determining which of these is the more correct is not important since both presuppose the same understanding of *shlh* (*sheloh*) and are equally messianic. Justin Martyr even charges the Jews with having changed this because of their anti-Christian motives.[8] The modern critics take this to mean "until he [i.e., scepter or ruler's staff] comes."

Further support for this traditional view of the passage comes from Ezekiel 21:32 (27 EB), "until he come whom the judgment belongs to and I will give it to him." Some argue that Ezekiel has Nebuchadnezzar in mind. If this were the case, there could have been no reference to the ancient prophecy, because the Shiloh prophecy could not have found fulfillment in the rule of Nebuchadnezzar. The judgment is not the judgment of destruction; rather it is "the government." The meaning therefore is essentially the same in Ezekiel as in Genesis. Some maintain that the Ezekiel prophecy is the older and the prophecy was introduced into the oracle of Jacob. Objection: now it would be impossible to believe that Jacob would have prophesied a fulfillment in the time of Nebuchadnezzar. Therefore, we would not expect a later Jew to inject this into the oracle. Ezekiel is explanatory of the Genesis passage and both are messianic. The word *judgment* in Ezekiel may show the connection. The word is not ominous but, in Hebrew, means something like "ruler's staff."

Then, too, attention has been called to the peculiar connection of the letters in the two passages. In Ezekiel (aSHer Lo Hamishpat), the important letters spell SH-L-H (*sheloh*). These are our objections: (a) in Genesis the subject is implicit, and in Ezekiel it is expressed, viz., *mishpat*. The form in Genesis appears to be abbreviated, as if it were a well-known prophecy. If Ezekiel actually refers to it, then he gives his interpretation of it (this is not so much an objection as simply a difference between the two). (b) The objection against it is that it leaves the appurtenance of the Messiah toward Judah unexpressed. Yet the context requires that this be expressed, i.e., it looks as if Judah will have to step aside for the one that is to come. The messianic statement seems to lose the inner connection of the prophecy as a whole. This would not be the case if one renders it as the first LXX rendering above. But this does not agree with the Ezekiel passage, which makes the subject refer to the Messiah and not to Judah. However, the difficulty is in making the subject specific;

i.e., Judah's ruler staff. We could paraphrase thus: "until he come to whom the Judean scepter and ruler's staff belong."

The newer view is that the word *shlh* is to be understood of the Messiah as the "Giver of Rest." The word is a proper noun, and the phrase would be rendered "until the Restgiver comes." Early authority for this is hard to discover. The earliest allusion is where Solomon is associated with Shiloh. This view is common in the modern schools, particularly those influenced by Hengstenberg. The latter finds references to support this rendering throughout the entire Bible:[9] "Prince of Peace" (Isa. 9:6); "King of Peace" (Ps. 72): "this one shall be peace" (Mic. 5:6—v. 5 EB); Messiah "rides upon the animal of peace" (Zech. 9:9); "man of rest" (1 Chron. 22:9); "he is our peace" (Eph. 2:14). But we object: (a) linguistic considerations are against it; as Ewald has pointed out, on Hengstenberg's view, the form should be *shiloi*. Hengstenberg responds by saying that this is an abbreviation of *shilon*.[10] Delitzsch counters: it should then be *shilion*.[11] (b) It would not express that Shiloh comes from Judah, which the whole tenor of the prophecy would require. To meet this it has been rendered "until Shiloh proceeds from him" or "until he gets his Shiloh." (c) The election of Judah is very important in connection with what is to come, and we would expect mention to be made of it. Mention is made of this only in 1 Chronicles 28:4. The three steps are given; therefore, we would also expect this. (d) The conception of the Messiah as bringing peace is so ancient and self-understood that the passages quoted need not depend on any particular antecedent prophecy. (e) The form of this interpretation, not having a suffix, the appurtenance of the Shiloh to Judah remains unexplained. Although the proper name takes no suffix, yet in some other way (i.e., "the Shiloh to him") this could have been, and should have been, expressed.

Lagarde's explanation is that *shlh* comes from *shailh* (*she'iloh*). Dropping out of the *aleph* is no fatal objection. It would be rendered "his asked-for-one" (from *sha'al*, "to ask"). Thus, it means one who is sought after or prayed for (cf. *sha'al* in 1 Sam. 1:27; "Jehovah whom ye seek," Mal. 3:1). Our objections are: (a) The term occurs nowhere, and this is all the more significant because it is a common appellative noun. *Shail* does not occur as a common adjective in Hebrew; it is not a proper name as the suffix shows. (b) This view leaves unexplained how *she'iloh* (with long *i*-sound) could have been changed in so many manuscripts to *shelloh* (without *i*-sound). The rendering of Jerome (Vulgate) and Eusebius is *shaliah* or *shaloah* = "the sent one." Eusebius connected this suggestion with John 9:7, where the Pool of Siloam is interpreted "Sent."[12] Jerome's version reads *qui mittendus est*, "to whom it was sent." The Jews have been charged with the falsification of this text by changing *shalual* into *shelloh* or *shiloh* because of their desire to eliminate the messianic meaning. We object that: (a) the charge of text-corruption is absurd because *shelloh* and *shiloh* are just as easily messianically interpretable as *shaluah*; (b) the *-oh* reading is found long before the Christian era in the LXX; (c) the whole view seems to have sprung from a misreading of the Hebrew characters on the part of Jerome and Eusebius; (d) the main objection, however, is that this view leaves unexpressed the belonging of the Shaliah to Judah (relation of the one "who is sent" to Judah) which is what the whole tenor of the prophecy requires.

The view that connects *shlh* (in the form *shaljah*, "afterbirth") with the idea of birth or the birth-relation of the Messiah. There are three forms of this view. First, "afterbirth" (cf. Deut. 28:56–57—Sheljah) is proposed because it suggests origin solely from a mother; i.e., no human father. Driven by distress, a woman will eat her own afterbirth or the child whom she has just delivered. *Sheljah* (Latin, *secundia*) designates the afterbirth. Onkelos gave it a metaphorical meaning, viz., the youngest child. Thus it is derived from *shail* and with the suffix would be rendered "my son." These views cannot be traced back very far, probably to the eleventh-century Jewish exegetes and, among the Christians, to Raymund Martin[13] (ca. 1270) and Galatinus[14] (ca. 1500). Christian interpreters obviously think of (1) the virgin birth, i.e., Shail connected with the second birth (viz., formed with the mother's seed only); (2) "youngest child" as a contraction of *sheliloh* from *shalal*, which means "to extract from the womb"; (3) "child" in general as a contraction of *shalj* with suffix to form "his child."

The objections against this view are as follows. Such a word for child cannot be found in Hebrew biblical literature, although such a word can be found in the Talmud and Aramaic. Thus, if such a noun existed in Hebrew, it is rare and could hardly have been a general noun for "child." While the presence of the suffix suits the purpose of the passage, the suffix ought to have been feminine on the first and second forms of this view above; "her afterbirth," "her youngest." Galatinus actually proposed to read thus. Yet there is no antecedent noun in the context for this. *Shalil* and *shajl*, if existing at all, must have been rare words in Hebrew. Why then would they be employed here? Neither *shalil* nor *shajl* gives perspicuous sense. The word *afterbirth* for son is inappropriate. Although it might refer to the virgin birth of the Messiah, it does not seem a fit way to express this thought. Delitzsch says it is too nasty.[15] The afterbirth may be capable of carrying the idea of a virgin birth, but it does not suggest it. Then, too, he could not have been called the "afterbirth" of Judah. It is for this reason that Galatinus suggested that we must read "her afterbirth"; but then "her" would lack an antecedent, and the connection with Judah would be lost. The idea of birth without paternity would be the only thing explaining the first form of the view above. This is hardly to be expected at this stage of revelation. While the idea of birth without paternity might be expressible in this form (i.e., "afterbirth"), it could scarcely be deemed discoverable.

Giesebrecht suggests emending the text *shlh* to *msheloh*, "his ruler" (from *mashal*, "to rule"—cp. Mic. 5:2; Jer. 30:21; Zech. 9:10). This is appealing because the Messiah is often described with some such term. The great justification for the emended text is clearness and smoothness. The *mem* is to be explained by the likeness between *mem* and *shin* in old Hebrew writing. The term would apply here because the Messiah is often called *moshel* (cf. Zech. 9:10). It must be admitted that this emendation yields good sense. Still a text that would have been so clear would not have been corrupted into such a difficult version. Thus, the perspicuity of the text on this view would raise barriers against permanent corruption.

My choice among the many and greatly varying interpretations is this. I resolve the word Shiloh, after leaving off the vowels, into the three characters *sh-l-oh*. Then *sh-* is taken as the abbreviated form of the relative *asher*; *-l-*, I take as the preposition *lamedh*; the *-oh* at the end of the word is the suffix of the third-person singular bearing the possessive sense of "his." Taken all together, this yields the rendering "he to whom." That this is not an arbitrary or prejudiced explanation appears from the passage in Ezekiel that must evidently be accounted for as a conscious echo of the Jacob-blessing. Ezekiel 21:27 reads," I will overturn, overturn, overturn it [i.e., the government of Judah], until he come, and there shall be nothing more, until he come whose right it is [i.e., who has a title to the government under my disposal] and to him I will give it." The mysterious characters *sh-l-o* reappear here. It is true, the subject to which, in each case, the relative belongs differs as between Genesis and Ezekiel; but it differs only in form, not in substantial meaning. In Genesis it is the scepter and the judge's staff held by Judah, while in Ezekiel, it is designated as "the government." That there is no essential difference here is obvious. The prophecy relates, in each case, to the "coming" of a future figure in whom is vested by God the right to reign under him.

True, a difference might be found in this, that the "until" seems to carry the implication that when the overturning is at an end and the proper appointee has appeared, all the previous bearers of the rule will have been swept aside and have vanished from the scene. The "I will overturn" in its threefold repeated form very strongly conveys this. And yet, in the usual connection of the words in Genesis, the "until" can hardly be understood in the terminative sense. The meaning cannot be that, as the objects of the "overturning" in Ezekiel disappear, so Judah, when the "until" gets into operation, will likewise be discarded by God.

This creates a difficulty, I say, and might furnish an instance against the identification of Genesis and Ezekiel. At least, if Ezekiel has quoted here, it would indicate that in his quotation he had not been quite faithful to the intent of the original from which he took the words.

But this difficulty is relieved by observing that the words spoken about Judah do not mean their "until" in this ominous sense, as concerns Judah. The sense is not that, however exalted in position Judah may at one point appear, he will at the last be stripped of such preeminence and his position given to another who receives the right to the exclusion of Judah. That could not be, because the entire statement is in the nature of a "blessing," and by means of forecasts of deposition from eminence, it is not customary to bless. The point that the prophecy intends to make is precisely the opposite. It might, in order to make you feel this, be paraphrased as follows: "the scepter and the ruler's staff will not be taken away from Judah until the decisive point will have been reached in his history where he becomes immune to losing them because that one of his offspring, that issue from Judah, will 'come' [i.e., will eschatologically arrive], from whom, in the nature of the case, and in view of his person, it is absurd to think that it could possibly depart, and that is the eschatological king of the future whose reign and possession of all his rights and emoluments is ipso facto eternal."

You will notice that thus understood, the "until" has no terminative, but a climacteric sense. It is not "he will rule until someone else takes the rule out of his hands and deposes him"; but it is "he will rule so long until at last the mysterious figure appears who, as descended from Judah, imparts the character of eternity to Judah's rule." Now while this undoubtedly points forward to the Davidic dynasty and its rule, it proves at the same time that this dynasty is here considered *sub specie aeternitatis* ("under the view from the standpoint of eternity"); for otherwise there would after the "until" exist no stronger guarantee for the perpetuation of Judah's rule than there exists at the time of speaking. The dynasty of David as such is subject to the chance of time and history. Obviously, in order to bring the prophecy into its full force, it must be assumed to contemplate or anticipate the subsequent promise of eternal duration given to David and his house according to 2 Samuel 7. But this is not the proximate purpose as it has to do with the tribe of Judah.

The principle to be declared is the unendingness of Judah's supreme position in the history of the people. In order to affirm this, the mention of the Messiah, or rather of the *Shelloh*, is introduced. The reference to the *Shello* is purely incidental. And yet, it is of greater value to us if it were of the nature of a direct messianic prediction. For in the latter case one might think that here lay the first acquaintance in revelation with the idea of the great King at the end. As it is, the very manner of introduction proves that Jacob and the people of his time were familiar with him and his eternity-rule. Something that is entirely unknown cannot be of use after such a fashion to help the expression of another thought. Evidently, *Shelloh* and eternity of dominion were synonyms to them. There is something marvelous in this, that God can avail himself of what, from a human standpoint, seems incidental to let break in upon man's knowledge fundamental principles of the highest potency. However, while this is not an introduction de novo ("brand new") of the figure of the eschatological king, this one feature seems to be new—that he will draw his descent from the tribe of Judah. When in the Apocalypse, he is called the "lion of the tribe of Judah," this is recognition and verification of the exegesis adopted by us.

So much for the personal element in this prophecy. The question, however, arises whether, besides this, we learn something in addition of the content and complexion of the final future state through which the eternity-character of what is predicted or implied will find its realization. We have already observed that to the *Shelloh* is assigned the obedience of the nations. This should not be weakened by understanding the word for "nations" that is used of the tribes of Israel. For in that case, there would be no universalistic disclosure in the prophecy. This is unlikely because the implication seems to be that precisely in this respect will Judah and his *Shelloh* be differentiated; that to the *Shelloh*, there is more in prospect than to Judah himself, personally considered. The precedence among the tribes was a great thing—infinitely greater is the dominion of the *Shello* over the world.

Apart from this one feature the question of how much is here disclosed concerning the makeup of the eschatological state depends on the way verses 11 and 12 are connected with the foregoing. Does the patriarch, after having spoken of Judah's issue as an important item in the prospects of the career of Judah, reach back beyond this to a further specification of the felicity of Judah? If so, then the fine description of verses 11 and 12 is of tribal interest exclusively. On this view, it represents Judah as a tribe of whom it is foretold that he binds his foal unto the vine (i.e., the vines in his territory will be so common as not to be considered too precious to bind animals to). The following words are in the same line: "he has washed his garments in wine and his teeth white with milk." Or does this picturesque description refer to the descendant from Judah who will rule in the eschatological era? Let us not too hastily say that a description in such terms is too physical, too sensual to have anything to do with the person or rule of the great king. The Old Testament is far more realistic in such connections than we are or deem it expedient to be. Even the prophet Amos, who represents the unmessianic concept of the state of the latter days, predicts something similar as is here recorded on the view of a reference to the final king. Amos says that "the days come wherein the plowman shall overtake the reaper and the treader of grapes him that soweth seed, and the mountains shall drop sweet wine and all the hills shall melt [i.e., with the wine-juice running down]" (9:13).

I personally incline to the opinion that verses 11 and 12 in Genesis 49 are descriptive of the eschatological state. We must assume in that case that the patriarch, through the introduction of the figure of the *Shelloh*, was deflected from the further portrayal of the blessedness of Judah as a tribe and, as it were, lost himself in the contemplation of the transcendent beatitude of the ultimate descendant of Judah. It would be something like "great Judah's Greater Son." Only this much should be added: if one chooses to be an uncompromising premillennialist, absolutely refusing to spiritualize and, at the same time, an adherent of the principle of prohibition, the literalness of the interpretation and the strictness of prohibition will come into conflict. For such a one it is better, and perhaps in general it is better, not to understand these two verses eschatologically, but as a realistic picture of the conditions under which the tribe of Judah lived in Canaan. Then there can be no conflict between principle and mode of life, for it is not open to contradiction that the people of Canaan did not proscribe, in the days to which the prophecy on this view relates, the use of wine, just as little as they forbade the use of milk, which is mentioned here in almost the same breath as productive of whiteness of teeth.

Let us summarize the material on the Shiloh prophecy. It is the first messianic deliverance in the Old Testament, and its messianic import is reasonably sure. It brings the Messiah in line with the elective process as illustrated in primeval and patriarchal history (i.e., Semites, Noahites, etc.), thus narrowing the field of messianic prevenience. Kurtz says that the emergence of the messianic figure is out of place here because it cannot be before Mosaic times.[16] Hengstenberg answers that prophecy cannot be chained to history.[17] Sufficient contact is shown by the narrowing-down process. To say that it could not have jumped from Judah to the Messiah is too rational because patriarchal history has a biographical character. It furnishes a necessary basis for subsequent messianic ideas in the Old Testament. Notice especially in the Psalter that there are elements not accounted for by the words revealed to David. Subjective poetry requires objective prophecy as its antecedent. It gives expression to the eternity of the messianic idea and makes it an eschatological concept.

The *ad ki* in the text has a climactic force, meaning up to that point and afterwards. The messianic idea appears wedded to the idea of universalism. Relative to this idea different renderings of the text have been offered; viz., "to him shall be the obedience [*ikhaah*] of the people"; Jerome (Vulgate) and the LXX suggest "to him will be the expectation [*prosdokia ethoon* equals *tikwaah*] of the peoples"; "to him shall the people be gathered" (*jikkaawu*, niphal of *paajaah*). All these renderings will fit into the context. Isaiah 11:12 even seems to support the last suggestion. But there is no reason to depart from the reading given. The word translated by "people" may mean "tribes," but "people" is preferred because the tribes have been sufficiently disposed of in the preceding. But other nations will render obedience, being prompted by friendly motives. Judah's reign will be by force, but the highest reign will be of him to whom there is spontaneous obedience.

What about the content of the messianic function: is it dynamic or static? That the nations will obey him gives evidence to the latter. It may be questioned whether Genesis 49:9 gives us any content. It pictures a lion, and Christ is called the lion of Judah (Rev. 5:5), but all that can be inferred from that is that Judah is descriptive of the Messiah. The contrast seems to be in the manner in which the two obtain rule, especially if verses 11–12 are applied to Messiah. If Messiah is the subject of these statements, then it is a contrast between his siege and the warlike one of Judah. The reasons for the messianic exegesis are that Judah cannot be pictured as a land flowing with milk and honey. Also, verses 11 and 12 show points of contrast with other messianic passages (cf. Zech. 9:7–9) and the nature prosperity is a standing messianic picture. Some think that this is too realistically natural (cf. Isa. 63). This naturalistic conception, however, is not modern, but very old, and can be traced in scholars throughout the ages up to Luther.

9

THE SINAI THEOPHANY

Like the deluge, God's appearance on Sinai contains an eschatological element. However, in the deluge, the negative destruction-idea of the world's crisis is brought out. Here at Sinai, the constructive, positive element of redemption is presented. This is further brought out by viewing it in its historical setting. In its context the eschatological significance is clear because it is the climax of the events of the exodus. These events were the redemption of Israel and are typical of the messianic redemption in the New Testament. The terms of our salvation are derived from this. Now the New Testament redemption has the inherent character of gravitating toward an end and this same feature must be sought in its typical forecast; i.e., the climax at Sinai is typical of what will happen at the end of the world.

This event is preceded by a judgment culminating in the judgment of Egypt. The plagues are preparatory to the final catastrophe, and they also serve as the last summons to repentance. A similar scheme is found in the prophets: Amos 4:6–12 enumerates famine, pestilence, war, etc. (cf. also Amos 7:1ff. and Hos. 9:7ff.). In Babylonian eschatology, this same idea is connected with the deluge.

This culmination is brought about by a theophany (i.e., God coming) and resembles the theophanic character that is everywhere theophanic. This in itself would not represent the end of the world, but this theophany bears an extraordinary character. We have here thunder, thick cloud, sound of trumpet, mountain of fire, etc. Some of these are to impress the people with Jehovah's majesty or the majesty of his law (cf. Ex. 20:20). But on the other hand, this also belongs to the legislation as a judging act of God by expressing the terribleness of the divine judgment of sin. The phenomenon of volcanic eruption is unique in this account. Even though this eruption was natural, it well serves its purpose because it is in the most terrible natural phenomenon. This extraordinary event furnished forever the setting of the final theophany.

It serves to bring the people to Jehovah (cf. Ex. 19:4). If any eschatological purport is inherent here, it signifies not only the final coming, but also the crisis. The theophany now becomes an abiding fact. Jehovah henceforth abides with his people.

The Old Testament associates this event with eschatology. When the prophets speak of the wonders of the future, they never link it with their own times, but always seek the analogue in the Mosaic period (cf. Jer. 23:7–8; Isa. 63:11–12; Hag. 2:6–7; Mal. 4:1).

In regard to the New Testament references, the trumpet of the resurrection of which we read in Revelation is the Sinaitic trumpet. Hebrews 12:18–29 parallels the Sinaitic and the final event along three lines: (1) the two mountains, the material and the spiritual (i.e., Mount Sinai and the heavenly Jerusalem); (2) the prophecy of Haggai is quoted in which we are told that God made the earth tremble ("yet once more will I make to tremble the earth not only, but also the heaven"); (3) there is a concluding word that God is consuming fire.

10

THE BALAAM ORACLES

The next personalized eschatological prediction is that found in Numbers 24:17. The seer Balaam here exclaims: "I see him but not now, I behold him but not nigh: there comes a star out of Jacob, and a scepter shall rise out of Israel, and shall smite the corners of Moab, and destroy all the children of Seth." It is evident that the representation makes Balaam peer into the distant future—"not now and not nigh." This insofar suits his historical position; for he stands at a sufficient distance in the days of Moses from the arrival of him who is called the "star" and the "scepter." But the remoteness is also sufficient, if the reference is assumed to be, not to the eschatological king, but to David either personally or to the Davidic dynasty. We cannot be sure, therefore, that we have here an eschatological prophecy, strictly speaking. It might be no more than a prophetic announcement of the Davidic kingdom without further messianic implications.

Critics of the modern school are not satisfied even with a modest residuum of what was almost universally regarded as an important eschatological *vaticinium* (prophecy). They think that it is, to be sure, a *vaticinium*, i.e., that wants to be considered as an ancient oracle concerning the epoch-making institution of Davidic rule over Israel; that, however, in reality it is what is called a *vaticinium ex eventu* ("prophecy after the event") dating from after the accession of David to the throne. This, of course, introduces the element of fraud into the oracle because it is antedated. It becomes, on this supposition, an instance of historical, contemporaneous glorification of the Davidic house projected backward into the Mosaic era in the form of an instance of false prophecy pretending to be the most solid and genuine kind of visionary inspiration (for the whole apparatus of a technical vision is here: the closing of the outward eye; the opening of the inward eye; the falling down of the seer into a trance). This would be fraudulence with a vengeance: the dressing up of what was well known to be fictitious with all the toggery of truth.

If there actually is here a glorification of David after this fashion assuming the pretense of prophecy or soothsaying in order to make its hero more glorious through throwing around him the aureole of far past prevision, the origin of the oracle would have to be confined to rather narrow limits. Nobody could have conceived the thought of such a glorification of the Davidic dynasty or David's person until the actual arrival of David upon the scene—in fact, strictly speaking, not until David's reign had attained to the rank of something epoch-making, which was not the case until sometime after David's accession to the kingdom. Nor, on the other hand, could the regime of the Davidic house have been depicted in such glowing colors after the reign of Solomon had come to an end, because immediately after that, the glory of the dynasty was so sadly reduced through the secession of the ten tribes that there could not possibly arise any further occasion to dwell on the excellence of David's house in such glowing terms as is done here. The advocates of this prophecy-after-the-event view must therefore date the quasi-oracle either to the latter days of David's reign or from the early days of Solomon's reign. For very early after Solomon's accession to the reign, the storm-clouds began to gather and the distant rumbling of the thunder made itself heard. At the end of Solomon's reign and immediately after his death the disruption of the kingdom of David laid all its glory in the dust, reducing it to such insignificance that not even an ambitious soothsayer would have found it worth his while to fabricate a grandiose Mosaic prophecy concerning it.

Still it is possible that within these narrow limits such a thing was actually done. If it was done, it would furnish us with an instance where we would be actually able to date the production of a false prophecy almost to the decade of its occurrence. There is no necessity for this. Nothing stands in the way of leaving David and Solomon altogether out of the reckoning here, and of believing that this is a veritable foretold description of the meteoric rise of the veritable eschatological king. He falls like a star into the field of Balaam's vision. That the one of his exploits mentioned by name is the smiting of Moab does not prove that David is the fulfiller of the prediction, inasmuch as later on, well into the time of the major prophets, and long afterwards, such a conquest of Moab appears as a standing feature of undoubted messianic prophecy. That the later Judaism did not think in connection with this oracle of the person of David, or of the dynasty of David, but of the Messiah personally considered may be seen from this, that the false messianic pretender in the time of Hadrian was named by the Jews Bar Kokhba, in dependence upon this oracle of Balaam. Afterwards, when it became plain that he was a false messianic pretender, they changed this title by a slight substitution of one letter for another into "Bar-Kozibah," that is, "the son of lying." Finally, I may remark that there is no warrant for tracing a connection between the star here spoken of as a direct designation of the Messiah and the star of Bethlehem, since the latter did not stand for the messianic person, being merely a (supernatural) indication of the place where he was to be found.

Thus detached from the Davidic person and dynasty, the representation does not, of course, mark an advance upon the point heretofore reached in the blessing of Jacob upon Judah. It may be even said that there is here a pause in the onward progress of prophecy toward its goal, since the blessing of Jacob had at least connected the messianic person with the tribe of Judah. In Balaam there is nothing to that effect. He speaks not of

Judah, but of Jacob and Israel as the circle whence the scepter and the star will arise. This is one more piece of evidence that his oracle was not composed in view of the splendor of the Davidic period, for had that been so, then it is hard to see how he could have failed to make mention of Judah.

There are seven utterances preserved in Numbers 23–24. The four longer ones relate to the destiny of Israel, while the three shorter ones touch on the destiny of other nations. The fundamental idea of these oracles is the distinctiveness of Israel. This is brought out in the first of the long oracles: "Lo it is a people that dwelleth alone" (Num. 23:9). This is not geographical isolation; it is an ideal distinctiveness. It is a religious distinctiveness that springs from a relation to Jehovah (cf. Num. 23:8, 21–23). The second part of the oracle (viz., "and shall not be reckoned among the nations") shows that the distinction is not political or racial, but religious. Thus, the oracle has an eschatological coloring. This idea is further substantiated by the fact that God is the subject of all the well-deeds toward Jacob (cf. again Num. 23). This is also recognized *ab extra* ("from the outside"), heightening its importance and suggesting world significance. Balaam is a pagan and he comes with this recognition. The prophecy is due to divine inspiration; some even make this here mechanical inspiration. There is here an objectivity of vision by virtue of its being viewed by a foreigner, which is very significant. This is all the more significant because Balaam is really hostile and would prefer to utter a curse.

There are two elements in this distinctiveness: (a) the static element, i.e., a supreme state of blessedness; and (b) the dynamic element, i.e., a historical destiny in which Israel will do great and unique things. The static element or element of condition predicts the prosperity of Israel from a twofold point of view: (1) Israel will become extremely numerous (cf. Num. 23:10—"who can count the dust of Jacob, or number the fourth part of Jacob"); (2) Israel will possess a fertile land (cf. Num. 24:5–6—"as valleys are they spread forth, as gardens by the river side, etc."). Note that these attach themselves to the Abrahamic promise of a numerous offspring and a future Canaan. The dynamic element or element of action is this: Israel blesses other people (cf. Num. 23:11—"thou hast blessed them altogether"; Num. 24:7—"and his seed shall be in many waters"; Num. 24:17—presents the predominancy of Jacob; Num. 24:9—"blessed be everyone that blesses him"). This reminds us of the third element of the Abrahamic promise. Abraham's promise, however, is expressed positively and this is more negative; nevertheless the thought is implied that Israel is to be a decisive factor in the world. Then, too, some of these clauses have a decidedly positive character.

There is a distinction between Balaam's objective position and subjective state to be taken account of here. First, the prophecy deals with the future of the people of God. Second, Balaam does not belong to the Israelites. He reveals strange motives. He stood in some relation to God because Jehovah not only uses him, but he stood prepared to be used by God ("I cannot go beyond the word of Jehovah, my God"—Num. 22:18). This is a sincere confession of his relation to Jehovah, which is not a magic relation. As to his subjective relation, the case is different. The way in which God deals with him and the presumptuous and pompous self-introduction show that he does not stand very high spiritually. David introduces himself in the same way in 2 Samuel 23:1, but the spirit is altogether different. Nevertheless, Balaam stood within the circle of God's supernatural revelation. He is perhaps a remnant of the original Mesopotamian element. Although subjectively they are different, he resembles Melchizedek (especially notice the names, *El Eljon* and *El Shaddai*—Num. 24:16).

The bearing of Balaam's oracle on universalism and eschatological destiny consists in this. Like Melchizedek, he points to the fact that the future of humanity is connected with Israel. Now, we must not overstress the hostility of Moab in this connection. Balaam's extraneous standpoint occasions the external form of the prediction, i.e., in terms of political process. This is further brought about by the political environment of the situation in which Balaam finds himself. There is here therefore a twofold interest, viz., one that is static and one suggesting an interposition of Israel in the world. This external form of expression may also be found among the prophets.

Some had bound up the eschatology of this passage with the phrase "the Star of Jacob," and when this was touched eschatology vanished. The star was David, and he fulfilled this prophecy when he won over the Edomites and the Moabites. The rationalists say that this is history in the form of prophecy, i.e., it is an interpolation interpolated after David's victory. But, we note, this is due to making this clause the determining factor; yet the eschatology can be deduced from the tenor of the whole passage. There are commentators who believe this passage to be eschatological and nevertheless interpret this star as referring to David. The eschatological and messianic idea are not identical. In an eschatological perspective, a human figure (David) may enter as a partial fulfillment. If the star refers to David, then we have his figure in an eschatological setting.

The distinctiveness is carried to its eschatological acme and is not to be sought exclusively in Numbers 24:14. Evidence of eschatological import follows. First, Numbers 24:14—"I will advertise thee what this people shall do to thy people in the latter days." The word *latter* occurs in Numbers 23:10 and 24:20. This might refer merely to the individual Israelite, but then the terminology seems borrowed from eschatology. Balaam represents the death of the righteous Israelite as enviable. Consider the various views of *acherith*. (a) This refers to the end of an individual Israelite. He will have a peaceful and satisfying end by retrospectively viewing the blessings of God bestowed upon him. But this is unnatural, and the context does not suggest a dying person. Even if it did, the source of gladness would be his numerous offspring (cf. the context). However, this is not true exegesis because the subject of the death is the righteous and therein lies the reason of his happy death. The righteousness of Israel is distinctive and this distinctiveness is projected into the future. (b) "The latter days" gives the proleptic hope. This finds individual parallels. After death does not mean immediately after death, but simply that Israel has a hope for something after death. (c) The first part is taken of Israel collectively and to put this individual-istically is strange. "Let me die the death of Israel" is then taken nationally. (*Righteous* is sometimes a proper noun for Israel; cp. the Psalms.) Thus, we have "let me die the death of the right-eous." But the difficulty lies herein that you then have the idea of a nation dying.

Next is the idealization of Israel's future in the absoluteness of the promises (cf. Num. 23:21, 23). According to verse 21, God beholds "no *aven* [iniquity] in Jacob, no *amal* [perverseness] in Israel." The margin offers "trouble" for "perverseness"; but then one is moral and the other legal. So translate "no calamity and no trouble" (instead of "iniquity and perverseness") by taking "trouble" from the RV margin and changing "iniquity" to "calamity," as the word *aven* may also mean "calamity." This suits the parallelism of the clauses, which suggests the disap-pearance of all evil and trouble, a feature characteristic of the es-chatological state (cp. the LXX, which reads *mochthos* and *ponos* [i.e., "calamity" and "trouble"] both in the political sphere). *Aven* seems originally to mean moral and *amal* physical distur-bance, but both have undergone a change. Nevertheless, both should be either moral or both political and then depict an ideal state for Israel.

"Surely there is no enchantment with Jacob, neither is there any divination with Israel; in due season it shall be told to Israel what God has wrought"—Numbers 23:23. The margin suggests " . . . against Jacob . . . . against Israel . . . . it shall be told to Is-rael in due season what God wrought." In this way, the paral-lelism is destroyed. If the meaning is, there is no enchantment in Israel, then the first half of the RV rendering and the second half of the marginal suggestion would make good sense together. Should the idea be that these things are futile against Israel, then the second half of the RV rendering and the first part of the mar-ginal suggestion should go together. Thus, either "no enchant-ment, etc. with . . . it shall be told what, etc."; or "no enchantment, etc. against . . . now shall be said: what, etc." The former is to be preferred because there is expressed in it that which has a direct bearing on eschatology. All practices of enchantment will be supplanted, and God will always and absolutely supply the information. Thus, it is descriptive of the perfect knowledge of God's purposes characteristic of the eschatological state.

The last group of four small oracles presents a program of development of the world-power. First, the destruction of Amalek is foretold, but the instrument of its destruction is unnamed. Second, the fate of the Kenites is next. They will be destroyed by Assyria (Asshur). Third, Asshur and Eber will be conquered by an Occidental power coming in ships from the direction of Kittim (Cyprus). Last, this power from the west will also perish. The range of the prophecy depends on the understanding of "Asshur and Eber." If these refer to two parts of Assyrio-Babylonian (or Persian) power before the time of Alexander the Great, then the invasion from the west is the Hellenic one under Alexander, and the vision reaches no further than the latter. If the two parts relate to the divisions of the Seleucid Empire after Alexander, then the power from the west means Rome and the vision reaches to them. (Eber means that part of the empire that lies beyond the Euphrates.) Destroyer of the Kenites is Asshur (Assyria or Syria); of Asshur and Eber (Assyria and Persia), perhaps Alexander or Rome. In either case, such a far perspective deserves an eschatological classification. Since it reaches far into the future and deals with historical facts, the critics remove this from the old Balaam stock, though they admit the antiquity of the Balaam oracles. There is nothing similar in the Old Testament prophecy except in Daniel, which, however, is more complete because in Daniel the kingdom of God is posited at the end (cf. Dan. 11:36). Daniel presents the rise and fall of one kingdom after another, but the kingdom of God will survive all. This is also in the background of Balaam's thought, but it is not expressed.

The interpretation of the personal messianic element in Numbers 24:17 is next. First, it refers to David; i.e., so the rationalistic critics view the reference to David and the Davidic dynasty. In other words, this is a prophecy after the event, given in order to make David's reign more glorious; so especially the reference to Moab and Edom. Actually, it is assigned to a late period long after David's reign. But this necessitates placing the oracle beyond David at a point where (on the critical view itself) already a greater figure than that of David was in sight (i.e., the Messiah) to whom then the words would be more likely to refer. The prophets in honoring David would not make the conception of his reign equal to that of Messiah. One cannot say that the star and scepter belong to the Davidic dynasty because they do not refer to a royal house collectively, but to a person—David or the Messiah. Bar Kokhba (after Christ) called himself the son of the star and pretended that he was the Messiah. The term refers to the Messiah; for the prophets always expect conquest of the nations in the messianic era (cf. Isa. 16:13; 25:9–10; 34:5; Jer. 48:24; Ezek. 25:12; 35:1–2; Zeph. 2:8; Obad. 1; Ps. 137:7). Jeremiah 48:45 also speaks in terms of the prophecy in speaking of destroying Moab. This is an analogy of Balaam's star of Jacob that will smite the corners of Moab.

The following are considerations favoring a reference to the Messiah: (a) emphasis on the kingship of Jehovah is connected with the exodus of Israel from Egypt; (b) messianic kingship is the only one that fits in after the emphasis on Jehovah's kingship; (c) the eschatological form of expression with the pronoun used points to the Messiah (cf. "I see him but not now"); (d) "star" stands for imperial greatness and splendor; so used in Arabic (not so in the New Testament and Old Testament). Bar Kokhba depended on this. Isaiah 14:12 is ironical; thus Gregory gave to Satan the name *Lucifer*, i.e., morning star.[1] Also the word for "coming forth" is not usual: it means to step forth at an appointed time. Connection with the star of Bethlehem is supposed, but that does not prove that it symbolizes a king; (e) a late author would not describe the coming of David this way. If the date is Mosaic, then it is possible to apply it to David; more so if pointing to Messiah (cf. how the prophet must strain to see him).

A compromise theory points to David as a type of Christ. We object that types are not predicted in the course of revelation. The narrowing down of Jacob, Judah, and David is not made known until they appear on the scene. The conclusion is that the prophecy is solely messianic.

The differences in this oracle from the Shiloh prophecy are: (a) it connects the Messiah with Jacob-Israel, not with Judah; (b) subjection of the nations is described more concretely and at the same time in a more limited way (cp. "the nations" [Gen. 49:10] with Moab and Edom here); (c) in Genesis 49 there is "voluntary submission" (*yikehat*, Hebrew); here, "obedience" is compulsory by conquest of arms; (d) the Shiloh prophecy is climactic; this is programmatic, i.e., a successive unfolding of history. The differences are due to the extraneous source of this prophecy. Balaam looks upon the Israelites as a unit and does not show tribal preferment. The form in which the subjection is expressed is definite. Moab is to be reduced. The issue is described in war terms. Balaam, being outside, is better able to survey the successive stages of the development of the world-power.

11

THE MOSAIC THEOCRACY

Here is the attachment of further eschatological revelation to reality. Thus far eschatology has attached itself to events and predictions, but now it becomes static in the theocracy in Canaan. Development of eschatological revelation is determined by the existing state of things. It does not grow out directly from previous revelation, but the fact that that revelation has born fruit in religion.

The eschatological idea influencing the constitution of the theocracy becomes dependent on the interaction of the type and the antitype. The future state imposes its own stamp on the theocracy, an actual institution of Israel. The theocratic structure projects its own character into the picture of the future. Heaven reflected itself on Israel and Israel became part of the future. The type inevitably influences the conception of the antitype. The future is depicted in terms drawn from the present, earthly, material reality. There is somewhat of the shadowy, inadequate character of the prefiguration that passes over into the description of what the eschatological will be like when it comes. The antitype impresses its stamp upon the theocratic structure and imparts to it somewhat of its transcendent, absolute character. The theocracy has something ideal or unattainable about it. Its plan, as conceived by the law, hovers over the actual life of Israel. The theocracy in the idea transcends its embodiment in experience.

Both of these partake of the character and limitations of the Old Testament. Israel fell short of the ideal at all points. This theocratic organization of Israel had something ideal about it from the beginning. It could not be attained. It hovered over the life of the people. For this reason, says Wellhausen, it is a product of speculation (cf. the kingship of Jehovah; the mixing of state and church; holiness of Israel; eternity of the covenant: all prints of the supernatural). The great principles and realities of theocratic life were embodied in external form. This was the only way to clothe the essence of the theocracy in a way that the Israelites could grasp. In order to keep the future eschatological picture in touch with Israel's religion these forms had to be maintained. The prophets had to give the essence in particular forms. Eschatological revelation is presented in the language of the Mosaic institutions. The New Testament first transposes it into a new key. Here in the New Testament it is spiritualized. In the Old Testament it is expressed in terms of perfection of the forms of Israel's theocracy. The holy city is center; offices, organization, peace, abundance, etc. are there, but this all is to be eternalized in the messianic era, and will be free of the vicissitudes of the present era. All this is the content of revelation.

Now, how can this be revelation and then yet be so dissimilar with the fulfillment? A distinction must be made between the substance and the form of revelation. The substance is eternal principles embodied in the forms as we know them. These peculiar forms are used because they are the most suitable forms of the time in which the prophecy was given. So far as God's intent was concerned, this whole apparatus was symbolical. Only the embodied ideas are to be fulfilled.

Now from God's standpoint, the prophecy and its fulfillment cover each other. But this is not absolutely true from the standpoint of the recipients of the prophecies. It is inevitable that they would be inclined to take the form and substance as a whole and project them into the future. This is true to a certain sense even of the prophets as well as of the people. Their subjective understanding is not adequate to the intent of God. Yet the revelation of God is to be measured as to its content by the intent of God, i.e., his words must mean what he would have them mean. The prophets grasped in and with the form the ideal substance, and did not clearly distinguish the two. For the same reason there is room for a difference between the subjective understanding of the people and the prophetic fulfillment. By what hermeneutical principle can we get at God's intent? By the New Testament teaching in regard to that fulfillment. It teaches us that the form is cast aside and that the substance is brought to light. The New Testament is necessary for the interpretation of the Old Testament prophecies, the fulfilled and the unfulfilled. It does not treat the matter mechanically, but organically, according to well-defined exegetical principles. The fulfilled prophecies revealed an organic, progressive unfoldment, and this may be applied to the unfulfilled prophecies.

There are, however, instances of literal fulfillment, e.g., the birth of Christ at Bethlehem. Yet this is not a concrete fact by itself, but an illumined idea, i.e., it is expressive of the idea that Christ will be born in the most humble circumstances. Now it is unwarranted that we should demand every detail to be fulfilled, for this would be a logical impossibility (e.g., the restoration of Israel, Moab, Edom, Ammon, etc. with their interrelations). Is Israel to be looked upon as a form or a substance? This opens a large field for spiritualization. This spiritualization is seen in the prophetic fulfillment recorded in the New Testament, and the beginnings of this may even be seen in the history of prophecy. Although none of the Old Testament prophecies are free from the Old Testament characteristic forms, yet occasionally the ideal substance breaks through. This is increasingly the case as the prophecies develop. This is true only in general because Ezekiel (later than Jeremiah) adheres closer to the old forms than does Jeremiah. The prophets begin to employ the external forms so as to imply the impossibility of their fulfillment, i.e., they are beginning to use them symbolically. Thus, Isaiah teaches that all nations will rest and worship on the Sabbath at Jerusalem; it is a physical and logical impossibility. At first, the universalistic view was expressed in terms of military compulsion and later in terms of free will induced by religious motives. Ezekiel still made the distinction between priests and Levi and predicted the continued ritual forms, but the older prophets had a conception of a spiritual priesthood. (Isaiah never mentions a priestly sacrifice in the eschatological picture, and Jeremiah 3:16 says that the ark will no more be mentioned because it has been spiritually fulfilled.) Also we find the idea of universal approach to God in Isaiah and Jeremiah.

To summarize this in other words: it was impossible for the people of that time to separate the essence from the form. The essence grasped in the form is different from the form being grasped at the expense of the essence. We find the picture of the eschatological state in terms of the holy land, Jerusalem, the rule over the nations, familiar offices and organization and rites, and temporal blessedness. Nonetheless, all this, while expressed in similar terms, was felt to be different from the present because it was represented as eternal. To the mind of God, all earthly apparatus employed is purely symbolical. To the people, and in part to the prophets, the symbolical nature was not always perspicuous. The prophetic understanding of the eschatological revelation was not the measure of its revelation-import to the mind of God, far less the understanding of the people. The problem is: How can the mind of God be ascertained apart from the intent of the prophet? This is to be solved only by reference to the New Testament interpretation of the prophecies. This applies to unfulfilled as well as to fulfilled prophecies because the New Testament does not proceed mechanically or by single cases in this matter, but enables us to fix certain general principles that all cases must follow. This applies not only to the form of Israel's life, but likewise to the problem of Israel's permanent or passing significance in the world of redemption.

The spiritualization of the typical began with the Old Testament itself. On the whole this was progressive although not a rectilinear development (Ezekiel falls short of Jeremiah). There was the gradual perception of the symbolism as such on the prophet's part (cf. Isa. 66:23). The typical theocracy remains behind the antitype in the lack of unification and offices. Another point by which the eschatological picture is influenced is that the various elements that go to describe God are distributed over various institutions and offices. The kingship and priesthood are not united in one order. The idea of the covenant and the kingdom is not carefully adjusted. And what is true of the verbal is also true of the theocratic prophecies. Sometimes even in one prophet there is a total absence of an attempt to correlate; sometimes only the kingship is mentioned and not the priesthood, and vice versa. Thus, the Old Testament is led to pursue these lines of approach separately.

12

THE DAVIDIC PROMISE

Here the intermarriage of the Davidic house and the messianic expectation is consummated. Still even here the terminology of "Messiah" and cognate ideas does not immediately appear; that follows later in the Psalter. Instead of this, we here make our first acquaintance with a conception that was destined to play a most important role in the revelation of messianism. This is the conception of divine sonship as applied to the Messiah. Let us note clearly how this is introduced. It enters in through the manner in which David's son (Solomon) is spoken of, and not only Solomon, but the entire succession of Davidic kings that are to sit upon the throne of David as rulers over the kingdom of Judah.

When God promises that he will in the future consider David's son as his own son and treat him accordingly (2 Sam. 7; 23; 1 Chron. 17), a momentous change is made by this, so momentous and far-reaching that it is hard to estimate the consequences without careful reflection. At first, it is true, there would seem to be no more in this than a promise of exceptional favor to the successive descendants that in the sequel will sit upon David's throne as his successors and the perpetuators of his kingship. We might be inclined to ask what is there specifically eschatological and messianic in this, for the singular number of the noun *son* in no wise indicates that one particular successor is referred to. According to the generally dynastic way of speaking, each descendant of David upon the royal throne is a "son of David" so that the mere phrasing of that would not bring us one step nearer to the messianic circle of ideas.

But on careful reading, we very soon perceive that there is a much deeper background to this, and it is this deeper background that supplies the messianic values. First of all, let us notice that in connection with the promise about this son of David the note of eternity is introduced and that this lifts it out of the sphere of temporal and relative happenings into the sphere of eternity and absoluteness: "I will set up thy seed after thee, which shall proceed out of thy bowels, I will establish the throne of his kingdom forever, I will be his father and he shall be my son" (2 Sam. 7:12–14). That is high-sounding court-ceremonial language, such as seems to have been more or less current in the royal houses of the Orient. It is addressed to the newly enthroned king in such a way that everybody knew full well that it was ceremonial politeness and not literally meant by anybody who spoke it or heard it spoken. Perhaps a trace has been preserved in the manner of address to the king which we find in Israel, "O king, live forever!" Anybody might say this if he was obsequious enough and nobody thought that anybody could understand this in a literal sense. Precisely that it was an accession formula of greeting applied to each new king must have proved to the king thus greeted that nobody meant to ascribe to him immortality or eternal kingship. Besides, there is the unqualified absolute way in which divine sonship is promised to David's successor.

The second half of verse 14, it is true, at first sight seems to be unfit for a messianic interpretation. It reckons with the possibility of the successor of David committing iniquity and there was, so far as we know, no time in which this was contemplated as possible in the eschatological king; for he stands for the new state of affairs in which all sin will have been overcome. But closely looked at, the words in question are not intended to stress that committing iniquity is unavoidable. Their purpose is rather to emphasize the divine favor to the future king; even though he should commit iniquity, God will not, on that account, take away his mercy from him as he had done in the case of Saul, but only make it the occasion for discipline: "I will chasten him with the rod of men and with the stripes of the children of men" (2 Sam. 7:14); that is to say, in moderation, "but my mercy shall not depart away from him" (2 Sam. 7:15). Although it was a promise clothed in this dynastic form of "the house of David," it was, of course, inevitable that there should be some in this line of succession who did not come up to the ideal set for a "Son of God." But rather than break off the line on account of that, God promises that his interposition will not be allowed to assume the form of destructive punishment. It will remain within the limits of chastisement which, if a father administers, does not break off the paternal and filial relationship and leaves open the way, in this case, of the line of David arriving at a point where neither punishment nor discipline is possible any longer because the absolutely perfect embodiment of divine sonship will have been attained and the sinless Son of God will appear on the scene. So conceived, the figure is, of course, eschatological; it passes beyond the ordinary imperfect behavior of the kings of Judah from the Davidic house.

Finally, there is the building of the house of God by the Son of David who is honored with the title "Son of God." It will be noticed that in this revelation David is not called the "son of God," but only his successor, Solomon. The proximate reason for this is that David was a man of war and blood, whereas the house of Jehovah should be built by a man of peace — and for the reason that the final kingdom must be characterized by peace and not war. But there shines through still another reason for this arrangement, viz., that the one who is to build the house of God cannot proceed of himself. He is not allowed to undertake this function unless previously he will have appeared in his own person as the product of the building activity of God. The interchange of the play between the two houses, that for Jehovah and that of David (in the dynastic sense), governs the entire construction of this prophecy. It is intended to reveal the principle that neither David nor any other mere man can construct the house of God. God must build first, then, on the basis of this, the successor of David, i.e., Solomon, can proceed with the building of the temple. This is so arranged to uphold within the frame of the prophecy the principle of the precedence of God's work before and above every human work in the realization of the consummate theocracy.

The subjective answer to these objective promises is found in the "last words" of David (2 Sam. 23). The core is in verse 5: "For is not thus my house with God? For he has made with me an everlasting *berith* ordered in all things and kept for all my salvation, and all my delight; shall he not make it to grow?" The English version here is not felicitous. It reads: "Verily my house is not so with God . . . although he maketh it not to grow." This rendering brings a dissonance into the words; the dubious statement would mark the opposite pole to the sublime assurance David means to express.

At the time of this promise to David (2 Sam. 7), messianism and the theocracy are not of equal antiquity in revelation so far as typical embodiment is concerned. Eschatology now attaches itself to the kingdom. It was given to David not at the time of his reign or his call, but when Jehovah had given him rest from all his enemies. From this positive vantage point, the eschatological hitches on. Although the messianic element from now on became central, its introduction was comparatively late, centuries after the founding of the theocracy.

The reason for this late introduction of the messianic conception is because the idea in institutional form was liable to gross misinterpretation, for it might be taken as a substitute for Jehovah's kingship. Thus, the kingship of Jehovah must first be impressed upon the people. In the last analysis, Jehovah is King. This precaution is also made in another way, i.e., first a bad, then a good, form of kingship is given so that the false and the good may be distinct. There is a twofold attitude on God's part presented in respect to this kingship, i.e. he disapproves and yet he complies. The critics say, here are two discordant accounts. We say, God disapproves of it as a substitution for his kingship. Saul's kingdom was not after God's heart due to both Saul and the origin of the kingship. The Davidic reign is approved, i.e., there is change from toleration to approval.

The religious aspect of the Davidic kingship lay in this: that human kingship became closely allied with the theocracy. In other words, the kingship, from the outset, has more than political significance; it is a religious institution. It is significant that it was after David desired to build the house that this promise was given to him, i.e., he must first be desirous of making his kingdom subservient to Jehovah's rule or kingdom. David's title to the royal office was established for good when he joined his rule with religious interests. There is a parallel between David's house and that of Jehovah. This thought gave rise to the desire of building a house for Jehovah. David's house is taken in the ideal, comprehensive sense, and therefore we must take Jehovah's house also in that sense. In both cases, the entire dynasty is mentioned.

The specifically eschatological aspect of the Davidic or theocratic kingship lay in this: the theocracy as a reality apart from prophecy (as a typical thing) refigured eschatology. David's kingship is lifted above the real thing because of its absolute element. Its features include: (1) its eternity. David's house will be eternal (cf. 2 Sam. 7:16). Verse 13 contains a similar prospective reference to Solomon. David recognizes it in his responsive prayer (v. 19). It is brought in connection with the eternity-prospect of Israel (v. 24). This relationship between God and Israel can never be broken. In the last words of David in this expression, this is presented in the same form. The idea of *berith* is carried over from the Israelite to the house of David (2 Sam. 23:5; Isa. 55:3). (2) The relationship between David's house and Jehovah is expressed in terms of father and son. Some say this expresses the peculiar love of Jehovah for the Davidic king. Others say the principle rests upon adoption. Still others suggest that the son of God is the Messiah.

Doubtless this latter contains much truth, but it is not sufficiently exhaustive. There is a close connection between David's desire to build a house for Jehovah and the sonship of David's successor. Notice that the father is the builder and the son the product of the builder. This is beyond the idea of adoption. Further, the son is in his turn a builder, for he will build a house of Jehovah. The connection between verses 12–14 (2 Sam. 7) makes this clear. To this adoptive element must be added the generative activity of God with reference to the son, and of the son with reference to the house of God. This has no metaphysical meaning in the first place, but it furnishes the first point of contact with the ontological nature of the son. Now the official and ontological sonships are not two heterogeneous things, but one leads up to the other, i.e., the official to the ontological. This suggestive supernatural element is pregnant with eschatological conceptions. The figure cannot be of a relative finite matter, but belongs to the process of the final issue of the fulfillment of the plan of God.

The theocratic king is to be a product of God. This is emphasized by the fact that the building of David's house must precede the building of Jehovah's house, the former to be the work of the Father. Therefore, David cannot, but Solomon must be, the builder. David cannot because he is a man of blood. The builder, the eschatological king, must be a man of peace and peace is characteristically messianic. For this reason, Solomon is typically more fit to be the builder. In the second place, David cannot be the builder of Jehovah's house because the builder is to be distinctly the son of God. (This is not said of David.) Now if Solomon builds the temple, it is thereby proclaimed that the theocracy is produced and maintained by the son of God and, in the last analysis, by God himself. The relation between God and king is put on a new basis (one of sonship and fatherhood).

Also, the relation between Israel and the Messiah is put on a new basis. He is no longer to be the product of Israel, but of God. It was thought that Israel was the son of Jehovah; this is now revealed to be untrue. The Messiah will not develop out of the consciousness of the sonship of Israel. It now abruptly appears that there is someone nearer to God than the Israelite, and through him all things must be mediated to Israel. This newly proclaimed sonship really gave Israel a more secure basis. The priority of the Messiah allows room for restoration in case of apostasy. If the relationships were coordinate, the same may happen to the Messiah. But Messiah's relationship cannot be broken, for it is more deeply rooted. The best illustration of this was the time of Jesus' crisis when the Israelites deserted him, and yet he was not rejected, i.e., his position does not depend on the Israelites. Thus, Israel does not build the Messiah, but vice versa. This is suggested by Jesus when he speaks of the wicked husbandman (Matt. 21:33–41); the cornerstone rejected by the builders (Matt. 21:42); his body as the temple (John 2:19–22), etc. Jesus actually speaks of his body as the embodiment of the theocracy.

In general, these ideas are applied primarily to Solomon. True, they are too great to be fulfilled in any other than the Messiah, yet there is no direct reference to the Messiah. Now we cannot infer that David applied this promise only to his kingship, or that he grasped the full import of the promise. He did understand it as something extraordinary, as is evidenced by the way that eternity is spoken of. It seems that this thought was not beyond David, viz., that a last successor will realize this. Although his grasp may not have been comprehensive, he surely included the Messiah-idea because that was in the Israelitish consciousness already before the kingdom (cf. the Judah oracle of Jacob). Now if Judah-prince is to reign forever, and the Messiah is to reign forever, the thought must have occurred to David that the two were identical. It is not to be determined whether he could come upon such a conclusion at once or by a process of meditation. Some think that he looked upon Solomon as the Messiah. Although this promise opened up the possibility of a person who was to be the Messiah, yet this, in all probability, was not applied to Solomon, because first a process of discipline must be introduced and therefore it must have been injected into the future.

("I will establish thy throne" must be taken collectively because the same has been said of David previously.) The general tone of 2 Samuel 23:3–7 shows that David drew the messianic inference.

The interpretation of 2 Samuel 23:3ff. ("One that ruleth over men righteously, that ruleth in the fear of God") is, on the modern interpretation, only hypothetically messianic. According to this view, the passage may be paraphrased: "if one ruleth over the men righteously, he ruleth in the fear of the Lord." This would not be strictly messianic. The true explanation is that the passage is figuratively messianic. It is a description of David's picture of the Messiah. Considerations in favor of this view are: (a) the whole setting and solemn introduction (vv. 1–3a) favor this; (b) the whole language is received from the Spirit of Jehovah (vv. 2–3a) and therefore we would expect more than a mere (hypothetical) idea; (c) verse 5 (AV) implies a special, extraordinary distinction for David's house—the interrogative is a strong affirmative and should be rendered, "for is not thus my house with God . . . all my salvation . . . shall he not make it grow?"; i.e., David could not thus congratulate himself and his house on the hypothetical principle that a just king will be prospered, for he had no assurance that his successors would always be just; (d) the "everlasting covenant" (v. 5) shows conclusively the final and eternal (i.e., eschatological) aspect of the statement—in other words, there is no hypothetical "covenant."

13

THE ESCHATOLOGY OF THE PSALTER

The Psalms are by no means devoid of eschatology as was at one time supposed to be the case. If, as is now extensively recognized, the speaking or singing subject is at least in some, perhaps in many, cases not an individual Israelite, but the congregation of the saints, then the presence of an eschatological element becomes a priori plausible. When the church as a whole gave expression to her feelings in regard to a great epoch that was approaching, or, as it seemed to her, impending, then we may be sure that there is some eschatological interest at stake. Even we would hardly voice our feelings in a hymn sung by the congregation about some approaching church supper or similar form of entertainment, however pleasant the latter might promise to be. The worshiping congregation of Israel sing "a new song" because their hearts are full of the "new things" that are on the wing with which the air is already vibrant.

It is here in the Psalter that the term *Messiah* enters into the eschatological vocabulary. This nomenclature of messianism does not have its seat in the prophets. The term *Messiah*, i.e., "the Anointed," is specifically proper to the Psalter. Only we must not rashly infer, when the Psalms introduce this term, that in each case the title has a technical messianic connotation. Such an inference would be warranted only if we assumed, as many do nowadays, that the Psalms were all composed after the exile. In that period there was no longer any king, and we would of necessity be driven into the eschatological sphere if a king or an anointed one were mentioned. As it is, we must reckon with the possibility that the Davidic king happening each time to occupy the throne may be referred to. Besides this, there is another possibility to be taken into account before we dare say with confidence that here is a prophecy of Christ as the Messiah, the eschatological King.

The view has been entertained that at some time before all the Psalms were composed, the messianic hope had been given up, not absolutely to be sure, but in this sense, that it had been transferred from the individual Davidic prince to the congregation of Israel, so that from that time on, "the Messiah" or "the Anointed" came to stand for the anointed congregation, the King who should be the head over this being entirely lost sight of. It is even alleged that we still can point out the passage in which this momentous change was first introduced. This is, we are told, Isaiah 55:3: "I will make an everlasting covenant with you, even the sure mercies of David." It is exceedingly unlikely that the prophet should have wanted his words to be understood this way. Jehovah could not very well have been represented as taking back his mercies from the house of David and, in doing this, in the same breath characterize these mercies as "sure." The new recipients of the promise would naturally have reflected that, if that was all the sureness it had meant for David, it might in the end prove just as delusive to them. But while such an exegesis of the passage stultifies itself, the possibility remains that in certain instances the name *Anointed, Messiah,* might have become inclusive of the people. This would not be a revocation of the original promise given to the house of David, but merely an enlargement of it. We must, therefore, in looking at the material in each case, remember that the term *Messiah* may sometimes be a name of Israel. It is purely a question of contextual evidence.

Now let us rapidly run over the passages in which the concept of an eschatological King has been found either with or without the technical name *the Messiah* (of Jehovah). First of all, we cast a look at the second psalm. This has now for some time stood in the center of the debate, not a few critics interpreting of the nation what is said of Jehovah, having anointed his King over Zion, having declared him his son, having given him the heathen for his inheritance, the ends of the earth for his possession. In itself, all this would not be impossible, provided it were not understood to rule out the original personal Davidic Messiah. But in the present case, what is not impossible in itself becomes impossible because the New Testament applies the psalm to Jesus (cp. Acts 13:33 and Heb. 5:5). Besides, the difficulty arises in this case that "the Anointed" is introduced not merely as such, but he is designated as "King." There is no instance, I think, in the Old Testament where kingship is predicated of Israel as a people. In being carried over from the Davidic ruler to the people as a whole, this representation would have become purely metaphorical since no occasion can be pointed out on which the ceremony of anointing was formally carried out with Israel. We may therefore confidently affirm that here the messianic office and title occur in the strictest eschatological sense.

The next passage for examination is Psalm 20:6, 9. Here, we have again "the Anointed" in verse 6, whereas the "King" in verse 9 may possibly refer to Jehovah. The sixth verse reads: "Now know I that Jehovah saveth his anointed; he will answer him from his holy heaven." And the ninth verse: "Save Jehovah: let the king answer us when we call." In this rendering of the English Bible, "the king" is a description of Jehovah who is addressed in the former half of the verse. Some, however, rearrange the words so as to make them read: "O Jehovah, help the king, and hear us when we call." This introduces either the contemporary king, or the supreme eschatological king of the future. In all probability, the former is meant; "anointed" could apply to either with equal propriety since all the successors of David used to be anointed, but the whole tenor of the psalm is so descriptive that it is difficult to think of something as yet wholly future.

In Psalm 18:50, we read: "Great deliverance giveth he to his king, and sheweth lovingkindness to his anointed, to David and to his seed forevermore." Here it seems clear that the "anointed" is a king in the succession of David's dynasty. When, nevertheless, the psalm is in the New Testament applied to and appropriated by Jesus, this will have to be understood on the principle of typology.

The twenty-first psalm, closely related to the preceding one, does not speak of "the Anointed," but merely mentions "the king" in verses 1 and 7. The reference is clearly to the theocratic king of the time when it was composed and nothing technically messianic enters into the representation.

Psalm 28:8, on the other hand, furnishes a clear instance of the identification of the "anointed" with the people. In verses 8 and 9, the parallelism of the verses requires this: "Jehovah is their strength, and he is a stronghold of salvation to his anointed" ("their strength" corresponding to "stronghold . . . to his anointed"); and this is borne out by the repetition of the same thought in a different form in verse 9: "Save thy people and bless thine inheritance: be their Shepherd also, and bear them up forever." Jehovah is the Shepherd, and the people are the anointed, i.e., the Messiah. So far, this is the only case where we have found the Messiah equated with Israel.

Psalm 45 is not a messianic psalm in the direct sense, although allegorically it has often enough been made to refer to the Messiah. It is a wedding song for the temporal ruler just married or about to marry. In its being turned into allegory, we might put it on a line with the Song of Songs with this difference only, that in this case the New Testament yields a justification for the allegory. For the author of the epistle to the Hebrews quotes from it when speaking about the superiority of Christ to the angels as follows: "Thy throne, O God, is forever and ever and the scepter of uprightness is the scepter of thy kingdom. Thou has loved righteousness and hated iniquity; therefore God, thy God, has anointed thee with the oil of gladness above thy fellows" (Heb. 1:8–9 with Ps. 45:6–7). "Has anointed" here relates, of course, to the theocratic Ruler. It is here not the idea of appointive anointment on which the technical term of "Messiah" rests, but an anointing in the cosmetic sense, such as belonged to a royal feast, whence it is also called "the oil of gladness." The Messiah proper is anointed with oil, not for gladness, but to signify the reception of the Spirit by him.

In Psalm 61 there may be doubt as to whether the psalmist speaks of the contemporaneous king exclusively, or of the Messiah exclusively, or whether perhaps after a typical manner, he sees the former as one with the latter. There is no reference in it to the anointing. Nevertheless, the strongest language is used with reference to the king of whom the writer speaks: "Thou wilt prolong the king's life; his years shall be as many generations. He shall abide before God forever." Possibly, this is not literally meant; for if it were, we should have to lift the king spoken of and prayed for out of the range of ordinary rulers. Probably, it is the language of court-ceremonial.

Psalm 63:11 calls for no more than a passing remark. It declares: "But the king shall rejoice in God: every one that sweareth by him shall glory." The last words mean that everyone swearing by Jehovah (not "by the king," although the Israelite can also swear by his king, if he feels so inclined) will rejoice. The "swearing" has its parallel in the preceding verse in the rejoicing in God attributed to the king; "rejoicing" and "glorying" are the same concept. The king will rejoice in God; everyone swearing by God will glory. This psalm, therefore, contains no technically messianic element. The term *anointed* does not occur in it.

Psalm 72, which comes next, does not contain the term *anointed* or *Messiah*. The king of whom it speaks is also a "king's son" (v. 1b). These two must have been both living at the time of composition. What strikes us most in the content is the absolute, unrestrained manner in which the virtues and extent of dominion of the king are spoken of in the sequel. The eternity of his reign is stressed: "They shall fear thee while the sun endureth, and so long as the moon throughout all generations. . . . Those dwelling at the ends of the earth are subject to him; all nations shall serve him" (Ps. 72:5, 11). One is inclined to say this must be the eschatological king to be sure as connected with his dynasty. Then why not make the psalm a downright messianic one? The trouble is that, according to verse 15, men are represented as praying for him continually. This is not decisive. The question is: What is the object of the prayers for him? We may not exactly put it in such words, but do we not pray at the present day for the success, as we call it, of the cause of Christ? A dependence upon God is doubtless implied, but that is not excluded even in the highest messianic concept of the New Testament. There seems to be no other alternative here than that between applying the strong statements directly to the eschatological king or finding here likewise the influence of the Oriental court-ceremonial language. Suppose we adopt the former, there still will remain an obscurity about "the king's son." And the psalm throughout makes the impression as though the figure with whom it deals were present to the writer's mind. Can that be due wholly to prophetic projection into the messianic future? I leave the question undecided. At any rate, there is no trace in this psalm of Israel being invested with messianic dignity.

After Psalm 72 comes 84:9: "Behold O God our shield, and look upon the face of thine anointed." It would but be obeying a natural instinct to take "shield" as the direct object of "behold," for this would make the sentence perfectly symmetrical in its two members. There would be in each half of it a verb and an object. The "anointed" (Messiah) would be synonymous with "shield," and this would be a most appropriate designation of either the contemporaneous or the eschatological king. Still we may not let ourselves be prejudiced by such love for symmetry; for in verse 11 Jehovah himself is represented as the "shield" of Israel: "For Jehovah God is a sun and a shield." In several other connections where "shield" occurs, it is a designation of Jehovah. Accordingly, we will have to construe it on the same basis here, viz., as apposition to the vocative God: "O God, who art our shield, behold, and look upon the face of thine Anointed." The first verb then has the same object as the second has, and the translation will read, after the manner of a climax: "Behold and look upon the face of thine Anointed." Besides the nation or the king, the high priest has also been proposed as meant by "thine anointed." This would carry the psalm down into the post-exilic period; for it was not until then that the high priest began to figure as, in the sense here indicated, the general representative of the people because there were no kings any longer. It is not a matter of heresy to believe in post-exilic, or even Maccabean Psalms, but here there is no necessity for it. In our opinion, the psalm under discussion is not a directly messianic psalm. The Messiah of God of whom it speaks is one of the successors of David, all of whom received the divine anointing at the time of their accession to the Judean throne. However, I do by no means feel absolutely certain about this. There is nothing to prohibit the eschatological references except that the standpoint of the writer seems to be that of the present. And to carry that through we should have to bring in the more or less precarious hypothesis that in the Maccabean period, some people believed that their Maccabean Savior was actually the Messiah promised to Israel from of old.

In Psalm 89 the "Anointed" occurs twice. First, in verse 38 ("But thou hast cast off and rejected, thou hast been wroth with thine anointed"); and in verses 50 and 51 ("Remember, LORD, the reproach of thy servants, how I do bear in my bosom the reproach of all the mighty peoples, wherewith thine enemies have reproached, O Jehovah, wherewith they have reproached the footsteps of thine anointed"). In the preceding part of the psalm, it is plain that the reference is to the Davidic promises that God seemed to have left not only unfulfilled, but to have brought into disgrace among the enemies of Israel. The covenant that God is charged with having broken is evidently the promise recorded in 2 Samuel 7. This covenant was to be according to the divine declaration made at that time, an "eternal" *berith*. And now, the psalmist complains, there is nothing left of it. It is to be carefully noted how in the mournful, melancholy description of all that this Davidic covenant stood for, terms are used that seem to surpass even the terms of 2 Samuel 7 in their sweep and splendor (cp. vv. 25ff. — "I will set his hand on the sea, and his right hand on the rivers, he will call God his father, and is made God's first-born, the highest of the kings of the earth"; and v. 36 — "His seed shall endure forever, and his throne as the sun before me"). All this is so superabundantly and so incomparably royal and lies so clearly on the line of the second Psalm that there can be no doubt about its reference to the ultimate successor of David — the Messiah.

At the same time, the figure of this eschatological Anointed appears to develop out of, and thus somehow melt together again with the last preceding occupant of David's throne, about whose misfortune and degradation all those complaints in the middle of the psalm are made, for he likewise is called "the anointed" (vv. 38, 51). Now how could all these misfortunes and all this contempt have been pressed into the life of a single descendant of David, the last one upon his throne? One cannot entirely escape from the impression that the psalmist, while plainly looking forward to the individual Messiah, has sought a sort of melancholy consolation in the thought that, after all, Israel is likewise God's anointed. All that the Messiah stands for in the line of hope and confidence was given him not for his own sake primarily, but likewise for the people to whom he is sent as Jehovah's supreme sacramental gift. It is precisely because, in the anointed, the people have been made to suffer the reproach of their faith that the sorrow expressed is as poignant and deep. This is a most touching trait in the concluding verses. The identification on the writer's part (and he speaks in the name of the entire people) with the Messiah has something indescribably sweet and tender about it. It sounds like an approach to the piety wherewith the Christian reflects upon his identification with Christ.

In Psalm 110 it is not the king as such, not therefore "the anointed" that stands in the center, but the priest-king in the combination of these two offices. About the messianic reference there can be no doubt, since it is vouched for, like that of Psalm 2 in several places in the New Testament, notably by our Lord himself in his dispute with the scribes about the Davidic sonship of the Messiah (Matt. 22:41–46). And he receives a title fully equivalent to that of the Messiah, since in the first verse David calls him his Lord and makes the promise involve his sitting at the right hand of God, i.e., the exercise of rule over the world.

Finally, we have Psalm 132. Here, there is first a reference to David's offer recorded in history that he will build a tabernacle for God. The tenth verse in the form of prayer speaks of the messianic "anointed": "For thy servant David's sake turn not away the face of thine anointed." And according to verse 17, in Zion, chosen by God (v. 13), he will make the horn of David to bud and has ordained there a lamp for his anointed and will cause the crown upon his head to flourish.

To this review of the evidence from the Psalter, I must in conclusion add one passage from outside the Psalter that nevertheless is found in a psalm, viz., the psalm embedded in the prophecy of Habakkuk. Here we read in 3:12–13 (after that magnificent description of Jehovah's appearance for judgment), "Thou didst march through the land in indignation; Thou didst thresh the nations in anger; Thou wentest forth for the salvation of thy people, for the salvation of thine anointed." Here it is obvious that "salvation of thy people" and "salvation of thine anointed [Messiah]" are simply synonymous phrases.

Let us now recapitulate what we have found "Messiah" to mean in the passages reviewed. The anointed can mean:

1. The "Messiah," i.e., the eschatological king, the ultimate successor of David as commonly understood when we speak of "the Messiah." To this rubric belong Psalms 2, 45(?), 72 (?), 84 (?), 89, 110, 132.

2. The dynastic successor to David occupying the throne of David at a certain juncture in history. Such a king would be the "anointed" in what we are accustomed to call a "typical" sense. Here belong Psalms 18:50; 20:6, 9; 21:1, 7; 61 (passim); 63:11; 72 (?); 84 (?).

3. The nation of Israel is called the Messiah ("the anointed") in two cases — Psalm 28:8 and Habakkuk 3:13.

From this summary, you may judge for yourselves how much or how little warrant there is for the sweeping verdict that at some later point in history the messianic title and dignity were taken away from the Davidic house and given to the nation of Israel.

Unlike prophecy, the nature of the Psalter is subjective. It is inspired, subjective response to objective revelation. Only at times is this distinction obliterated, especially when the psalmist takes his stand in the future. As a response to the objective (i.e., prophetic, etc.) eschatological ideas, it is full of eschatology. It may in that way even give us new eschatological material, being responses to ideas not recorded. It also teaches us the manner in which the objective eschatological material should be assimilated for practical use. That there should be eschatology in the Psalter follows from the eschatological use of the Psalms. With a few exceptions, they all express the collective, subjective desires and emotions of the congregation of Israel. Even originally, it was a collective hymnal that received the sanction of God and is therefore God's Word. The majority of these collective Psalms have a bearing on the extent of eschatology. They hope for a change for Israel. A crisis in Israel was always considered eschatological.

The eschatological character of the Psalter is evidenced by definite expressions:

a. There are references to a new song (Pss. 33:3; 96:1; 98:1; 144:9; 149:1), new things, new creation, or new name (cf. also Isa. 42:9–10; 62:2; 65:17; 66:22; Rev. 2:17; 21:5). These conceptions are all connected with the fulfillment of God's plan.
b. There is a reference to "set time" (cf. Ps. 75:2—[75:3, RV]; 102:14—[102:13]; and Hab. 2:3).
c. There is a definite fixed program and the implication that there is a plan organically linking the previous works of God with the present and future, eschatological events (Ps. 77:10ff.; 138:8—"perfect that which concerneth me"; "forsake not the work of thine own hand").

140

d. There is reference to judgment being "written" (cf. Ps. 149:9).

e. "Morning" in Psalms 46:5; 49:14; 130:6 (cf. Pss. 59:16; 112:4; 118:27; 143:8; Hos. 6:3; Isa. 17:14; 21:11–12) suggests the break (dawn) of the great day of Jehovah. The English version translates it incorrectly "right early."

The Psalter's eschatological aspect is apparent in general expressions whose eschatological aspect is supported by the context: arise, Jehovah (i.e., for judgment); be exalted or lifted up, Jehovah; awake, Jehovah; speak out or be not silent; be not far off; stir up thy might; restore; finish; heal or quicken; redeem (positively eschatological); save; be gracious; snatch out; do justice. All these seem to be appeals for Jehovah to bring about a crisis.

The content of the Psalter is eschatological and messianic. We consider here the eschatological material in its dynamic aspect. Notice first the emphasis upon the kingship of Jehovah. As King he judges and rules. The following are a few of the Psalms in which this is very pronounced: 22:29 (28); 47; 93; 96; 97; 99; 146. The victory hymn in Exodus 15:1–18 conveys the identical thought. These may be explained from the thought that they are processional hymns or perhaps derived from the ancient custom of carrying the ark. At any rate, they seem to celebrate a military event. The eschatological throne is not on earth, but in heaven, and this thought reveals what is really meant by judging and subjugating nations, i.e., the kingship is to be absolutely universal (cf. Pss. 47:2; 48; 96–99; 146; also 2 Kings 11:12).

Psalm 93 is peculiar in that it introduces God as King, but treats his omnipotence over nature. It shows God's control over nature at the creation, i.e., from chaos to creation, and now this omnipotent act of God will repeat itself. Notice the change from past to future tense in verse 3. The principle in general eschatology is repetition of great events. Figuratively the idea of Psalm 93 is expressed in Psalm 29:10, where Jehovah is presented as sitting as king of the flood.

The form in which the judgment will be executed is theophany. This is not merely a prerequisite, but judgment is accomplished in and by his appearance (theophany). The judgment of destruction in the old forensic sense is a summary of procedure, i.e., sentence and execution are one. This is often described in terms of a thunderstorm (cf. Pss. 78:48; 77:18; 81:7; 29:3).

In another form the judgment is presented as Jehovah giving a cup to drink (Pss. 60; 75). Psalm 60:3 tells us that Israel itself must drink. The prophets and psalmist speak of a cup of wine and one of poison, both culminating in the same condition. This is perhaps due to the fact that the words *wrath* and *poison* are identical in Hebrew. Now the English translation mentions two poisons, wormwood and gall, and the effects ascribed to these (such as staggering, fainting, sickness, etc.) are the same as those ascribed to wine. Poison cup is probably the original idea and the cup of wine is an adapted usage. A better explanation is perhaps that the poison cup has here been changed into a wine cup ironically. Wine cup in a specific religious sense is of the eschatological meal. It is one of refreshment and has been changed to one of death. The eschatological meal is known to the prophets (cf. Isa. 25) and they changed it ironically (cf. Zeph. 1:7–8; Ezek. 39:17ff.). In the New Testament, the figure of the cup as one of life and also of death also appears in Matthew 20:22ff.

The element of forensic judgment is present in Psalms 1:5; 7:7ff; 9:4ff. According to some exegetes, there is additional forensic judgment upon superhuman beings (Pss. 58; 82). They propose a text-emendation in Psalm 58:1–7, "Do ye indeed, O gods [*elim* instead of *elem*, i.e., "in silence"] speak righteousness?" They suppose these "gods" to be the angels who rule the heathen nations (cp. Deut. 4:19; 32:16–17; Dan. 10–12). Further, they note that angels elsewhere are named "gods" or "sons of gods" (cf. Ps. 8:6 [5]; 29:1; 89:6; Job 1–2). But the context of Psalm 58 speaks against this view. The judged are "the wicked" over against "the righteous" (vv. 3ff.). Further, against the angel hypothesis, the judgment is described as "washing feet in blood" (v. 10). Therefore, the address of these wicked heathen rulers as "gods" and "sons of gods" is to be explained as an ironical reference to self-deification. In Psalm 82 the question is further decided by the manner of judgment, i.e., death results for the judged (v. 7), which the Old Testament never brings into connection with superhuman beings. "I said ye are gods" (v. 6) here also suggests irony. Note the manner in which the judgment shall be accomplished. The imagery of war is relatively absent in the realistically conceived judgment (cf., however, Ps. 35). The terrors are those of nature rather than those of war (cf. Ps. 18).

Preceding the judgment, the final attack of the nations upon Zion appears in Psalms 2 and 110 (both Messianic), 48, and 149 (generally eschatological). This scene of the attack upon Zion is detached from the background of contemporaneous history; it is a fixed item in the eschatological program. So also in the prophets, it is not born out of historical developments, but rather is antecedently known and lends form and language to their historic forecasts.

The eschatology of the Psalter is apparent in the restoration of the theocracy and the return of the captivity (Pss. 60; 111:6). Israel recovers its land; other land is acquired by Jehovah. Notice how the inheritance is spiritualized in Psalm 16:5ff. On the return of the captives, compare Psalms 126:4; 68:22; 85:5–6 with the liturgical appendix to the fourth book of the Psalter in Psalm 106:47 (cf. 147:2).

The vindication of Israel is eschatological. The charge of self-righteousness leveled against the Psalter is usually due to a failure to understand this idea. Israel is right over against the enemy—not over against Jehovah (cf. Pss. 4:1–2; 5:8ff.; 7:9ff.; 9:4ff.). The psalmist appeals jointly to Jehovah's lovingkindness and righteousness (Pss. 119:40–41; 143:1–2).

The universalism of the Psalter appears in the conversion of the nations to the service of Jehovah. This concept is approached: (1) through the kingship of Jehovah (Ps. 97:1, 6); (2) through the prospect of universal peace (Ps. 46:9); (3) through the principle of monotheism (Pss. 78; 82). All of these contain the germ of the working out of the doctrine of universalism. Also, there is the direct summons to the outside world. However, this is poetic and not actual missionary propaganda. There are varying degrees of spirituality in the working out of the idea of universalism.

Appendix: Additional Passages from Vos

1. . . . prophecy something more than bare, undisciplined skill in expounding single passages, turning them to a certain preconceived account, more than acquired gift for atomistic scholarly exegesis; it requires that much rarer gift of sufficient historic sense to transport oneself into the consciousness of the nascent church of the New Testament and to gather from its sense of living halfway in the fulfillment and out of the fulfillment the knowledge of what the prophecy, if it was intended to fit into this fulfillment, must have really meant *e mente Dei* ("from the mind of God"). This is a method of sounding the deep waters of the prophecy and bringing up from this depth the kernel-treasures of its original divine conception. . . . Jeremiah 30:24.

2. For determining who is meant by "thine Anointed," all depends on the construction of this verse (Ps. 84:9). The two possibilities between which we must choose are the following: either "shield" stands in apposition to the vocative *God*, which yields: "O God, who art our shield, behold." The verb *behold* then remains without an expressed object and this unexpressed object will have to be supplied from the second clause of the sentence, where it appears in the phrase *thine anointed*. It will be noticed that this rendering, while by no means compelling, yet leaves open the reference of "anointed" to the nation. Or "shield" has the place of the object to the verb *behold*, yielding: "O God, be-

hold our shield." This deprives "God " of the appositive name *our shield* and it carries with it the conclusion that "shield," being the object of the verb, becomes an exact parallel to the object of the second clause, "thine anointed." Since the suffix *our* distinguishes the speaking people from the shield, by force of parallelism the same will follow in regard to "anointed." The latter then bears the relation to the people that a shield bears to those whom it protects. The facts seem to us to speak in favor of the latter interpretation, although it must be admitted that something can be said in defense of the former. In the first place, there is the symmetry of the parallelism, which is perfect on the former view—"behold" and "look upon" on the one hand, and "shield" and "anointed" on the other hand, corresponding to each other. In the second place, the position of the words in the first half of the verse in the original renders this interpretation not only the more natural, but well-nigh the inevitable one. This Hebrew word sequence is "our shield, O God, behold." Had "shield" been meant as apposition to God, its natural place would have been not before, but after the word *God*. Among modern expositors deciding in favor of "shield" being objective case may be named the following: the Leiden translation and Duhm;[1] but the majority, including Valeton,[2] Baethgen,[3] Stark,[4] Wellhausen,[5] and of an older time Hengstenberg,[6] construe in the other way without, of course, thereby all implying that anointed means the nation, as Hitzig[7] and Wellhausen do. Over against this array of commentators may be placed the unanimous testimony of LXX, Jerome, Symmachus,[8] Aquila,[9] the Syriac Version, the Targum,[10] the Hebrew accents: all of which take "shield" as an objective case. The main argument. . . .

3. . . . the prominence of the note of worship and of making pilgrimage to the sanctuary might seem to incline one that way, especially when post-exilic origin is decided upon (so Olhausen as cited by Baethgen).[11] For the main point at issue, this makes no difference. Whether the reference be to King or High Priest, the distinction of the Anointed from Israel is on either view certain.

4. . . . sense as our Lord declared him to be a God not of the dead, but of the living (Matt. 22:32). There is a real correspondence in this respect between the large movement of redemption, taken as a whole, and the enactment of its principles on a smaller scale within the history of Israel. As the Second Adam is greater than the First and the paradise of the future more glorious than that of the past, so the newborn Israel to the prophet's vision of the eschatological future endows the people with far nobler attributes and richer blessedness than were possessed by the empirical Israel of the past. Even if the content of the hope were not transcendent, as it immeasurably is, even then the ascription to it of eternal duration and the removal of every fear of future decrement or deterioration of it would place it in a category altogether by itself. And in the last analysis both features, that of transcendent richness and of endlessness of possession, are derived from the vividly realized, absolute character of God. The prophetic eschatology is not only God-centered in the usual acceptance of the word; it is the very image of the divine character reproduced in the highest and most noble form of created existence.

The inadequacy of the scheme that would make the wealeschatology of the prophets the more balancing counterpart of the acute experience of woe in the present is also evidenced by this: that it has driven its advocates into denying the authenticity of the eschatological material of this absolute type which the prophetic writings contain. It is not merely the makeup of the material that has exposed it to suspicion, because its optimism seems to belie the pessimism with which the critical theory has overlaid the prophetic consciousness. To an even stronger degree, it has evoked doubt as to its genuineness by the abruptness with which, in many instances, it is joined to the most unqualified announcements of woe without the intermediate link of a solemn summons to repentance. All the external evidence with which it is attempted to buttress this critical verdict is quite insufficient for supporting it. Support for it can come only from the critical construction of the divine righteousness as a righteousness that left no room for the element of grace. This, however, is a construction which bears its doctrinaire character on its face. That God cannot show grace without previous man-wrought repentance is a philosophical promise, not an induction from the material as such.

5. . . . Ahaz: nine months from to-date there will be occasion for a woman to call her just-born child "God is with us" (Isa. 7:14), because she and others greet at that juncture its approaching or actual arrival that the name-giving implies. It will be further observed (and this is a thing frequently overlooked by advocates of the chronometrical interpretation) that in order to safeguard the accuracy and efficacy of the sign, or at least to secure for it conspicuous clearness, the *alma* should have been known or generally recognizable as one recently married and consequently not having born and raised children before. For that again would have thrown the whole structure of verifiable time-fixation out of gear. The prophet, however, adds two further time determinations to the one connected with the birth. The one attaches to the time when the child knows to refuse evil and choose good (Isa. 7:15), i.e., the time of beginning puberty, generally speaking. The other attaches to the age of the child before it will have attained that age and faculty of discrimination. At the latter point, the lands of Syria and Ephraim shall be forsaken (Isa. 7:16), that is, fallen prey to devastation such as will render them unable further to molest Judah. At the former point, when the state of discrimination is reached, the child will eat butter and honey, which means he will find nothing of the ordinary food supply in the land to be nourished upon, because cultivation of the ground has ceased. Only a small degree of dairy production will remain and this, together with the honey stored up by the wild bees in the wilderness, will have to sustain the child at that age. These two successive points then relate to the devastation of the land in the northern regions of Ephraim, which so long as it has not touched Judah could afford the name-giving woman a just occasion for the Immanuel-cry of joy, and then to

the immediate sequel of the involvement of Judah in the disaster. That the prophet means to include the disastrous fate of Judah in the symbolism of the life-experience of Immanuel may be inferred from verse 17: "Jehovah will bring upon thee and upon thy people and upon thy father's house, days such as have not come from the day that Ephraim departed from Judah, even the king of Assyria."

The context, however, makes a still further use of the inherent significance of the name *Immanuel*. He puts it upon the lips of Jehovah himself in 8:8. . . .

6. . . . The first passage of this kind is Micah 2:12–13, reading:

> I will surely assemble Jacob all of thee; I will surely gather the remnant of Israel; I will put them together as the sheep of Bozrah, as the flock in the midst of their fold: they shall make great noise by reason of (the multitude of) men. The breaker is gone up before them; they have broken through, and have passed through the gate, and are gone out by it; and their king shall pass before them, and the LORD at the head of them.

The main ground on which the majority of critics have denied the Micaian origin of this passage consists in this, that the Babylonian exile seems to furnish the only possible background for its import. There occur a few other passages in Micah that have for their motif the same thought of a comprehensive captivity and dispersion of the people (cf. 4:6, 10; 5:3; 7:12). The question confronting us in the interpretation of these pieces relates to the actual (as distinguished from the visionary) out of which they are spoken. Do they presuppose the Babylonian captivity, or are they explainable out of an earlier situation? To the average reader this alternative might seem to be identical with the alternative either from a later writer or from the prophet Micah's own hand. This, however, overlooks a third possibility; viz., that Micah might have projected himself, or in a visionary experience been psychically transported, into a time later than his life-time or the period of his prophetic ministry. It is unfortunate that the position assumed by the critics in this matter of diagnosing a case of captivity-production has so invariably brought with it the verdict of nonauthenticity. This state of affairs has prevented some conservative expositors from keeping an open state of mind on the problem of what was the actual power of prophetic self-projection in time through the fear that every discovery or recognition of Babylonian-captivity provenience brought the exegete inevitably near to or within the critical camp. There is no necessity of fear in this direction. Modern criticism has not yet been able to rid itself of the idea that prophecy was bound, in this small sense, to the limits of its own contemporaneous life-experience. To some extent, this is due to the preconception that prophetism was a literary sort of production to the reading to which the skillful exegete must bring all his canons of clear coherence. . . .

7. A footnote: The New Testament references to Bethlehem are: Matthew 2:1; Luke 2:4, 15. Strange to say, in none of these three passages is there any reflection, at least explicitly, upon the prophecy of Micah (5:2). Even Matthew, so fond usually of pointing out items of fulfilled prophecy, does not reflect upon this patent instance here. Did he think the meaning of the prophecy so universally acknowledged as to deem reminder of it superfluous here, while in other cases of a more recondite nature, he had the opposite feeling? That the prediction of the place was known to him and not only to him but to others including Herod is implied in the direction to . . .

8. . . . what offset, however, by the occurrence of the phrase "in the days of old ['olam]" (Mic. 7:14) to designate the time when this former feeding of the flock in Transjordanic pastures took place. "Days of 'olam" could easily be deemed a chronological overstatement on the part of one who lived and labored in the times of Jotham–Hezekiah. The surroundings of the pas-

sage are not overfavorable to the hypothesis of proleptic vision, for they constitute a prayer, such as would most naturally relate to the present or the past of the praying subject and bear upon present distress and relief. The critics think that assignment to an exilic or post-exilic date is inevitable because the prayer is in the tone of Deutero-Isaiah. Perhaps what the two have in common is not so much the earmarks of any particular literary style, but the unmistakable symptoms of the very language employed in all true, tender prayer, no matter whether on the lips of Isaiah or those of Micah, the remainder of whose book bears witness to his acquaintance with prayer. This particular effusion of soul is more a precursor of the prayer-episodes in Jeremiah than of the high flights of poetry in the so-called Deutero-Isaiah.

9. Zechariah. The prophecy that comes down to us under this name consists of two parts clearly marked off from each other by their peculiar style and import. Of the fourteen chapters composing it, the first eight bear an apocalyptic impress. Here we meet with "night visions" as in Daniel and horses run across the field called up in trance to the prophet's inward eye. In the other section comprising chapters 9–14 of the book, the more familiar mode of hortatory address, distinctive of the older, pre-exilic prophecy is employed. The subject matter revolves around the topic of sin, judgment, repentance, deliverance, restoration. This difference between the two sections of the book has given rise and lent a degree of countenance to the hypothesis of a difference in dating between the two constituent parts. And, strange to say, here the well-known divisive method pursued assumes the form of not post-dating, but of pre-dating the material exscinded from the traditional book. While chapters 1–8 are believed to reflect the actual historical situation of Zechariah, the remainder (chapters 9–14) are pushed back into the pre-exilic period. Within these limits, a distinction is further made between an earlier prophecy contemporary with the time of Hosea (viz., chapters 9–14) and a later one dating from the time of Jeremiah (chapters 12–14). This division cannot be rejected or accepted on the ground

of biblico-theological or eschatological principles alone. It should remain a problem for unprejudiced examination of the criteria applied. Not a few conservative exegetes, like Orelli, have in this case felt constrained to accept the proposed bisection.[12] The latter ought not to be confounded with the far more serious methods of Stade[13] and others, who assign the entire second portion of the prophecy to various post-exilic dates considerably later than the era of Zechariah. On the several aspects and merits of this critical problem, we must refer the reader to the commentators. The divisive treatment took its point of departure from the fact that Matthew 27:9 (in its account of what was done with Judas's betrayal-money), quotes the words about its having been devoted to the purchase of "the potter's field" as a fulfillment of a prophecy of Jeremiah. In our text of the book of Jeremiah neither these words, nor the occasion on which they are represented as having been uttered, occur; whereas both occur in Zechariah, a circumstance from which the inference seems justified that the first evangelist must have found them there.

Addressing ourselves, then, first to the "night visions" and endeavoring to appraise their eschatological import, we note first of all that they consist of seven distinct pieces dealing with the following subjects:

1. the apocalyptic horsemen (1:8–11);
2. the four horns and the four blacksmiths (or carpenters) sent to destroy them (1:18–21);
3. the glorious rebuilding and restoration of Jerusalem and Judah (2);
4. the distinction conferred upon the priesthood in the person of Joshua (3);
5. the episode of the golden candlestick (4);
6. the picture of the flying roll illustrative of the curse and of its removal by means of the ephah in which the woman sits (5);
7. the solemn coronation of Joshua as high priest in the presence of Zerubbabel (3–4).

As regards the scene of the apocalyptic horsemen, this is usually regarded as one of the outstanding favorite symbols of apocalypse. Still, the distinctive variation within the limits of this symbolism ought not to be overlooked. First, one appears called "a man" riding upon a red horse and standing among the myrtle trees on the slope of the valley (1:8). Distinct from this "man" is "the Angel" (1:9) who communes with the prophet; i.e., interprets to the latter's mind the successive elements of the vision as they unroll before the latter's inward eye in the trance (vv. 11, 14). Both "Angels" are superhuman figures, and yet "the Angel of Jehovah" among the myrtle trees, commanding and summoning to report the variously colored horsemen under him, is distinctly designated as "the man" (v. 10). If both "Angels," the Angel-Interpreter and the Angel-calvary-captain, are superhuman, they are nevertheless distinct, since the one addresses the other and solicits an answer from him. The answer to the prophet's inquiry "Who are these, my Lord?" (1:9) is obtained not directly from the Angelus Interpres, but indirectly from the Angel-captain over the horsemen. The gist of the answer thus obtained by the prophet is that the riders under the Angel-captain have executed their function; viz., that of controlling the earth, and report everything as being quiet. The patrolling appears as a search for eschatological indicia of the impending crisis. Jehovah, however, desiring, as it were, to guard against a mistaken inference from this reported quiescence, declares: "I was displeased with the heathen that are at ease" (1:15). And as a specific reason for this state of mind on God's part is given the following, "I was but a little displeased [i.e., with my people], but they [i.e., the heathen] helped forward the affliction [i.e., of Israel]." The upshot of the matter is: the silence in the earth reported by the patrol-riders bears a twofold significance. On the one hand, it is the silence of "the not yet." On the other hand, it is the silence of "presently." The divine intent remains unalterably fixed, while the crisis of its maturing is as yet delayed. The reported "silence" is, as it were, the oppressive stillness upon the atmosphere that immediately precedes the bursting forth of the thunderstorm of the judgment. And joined to the latter, as immediately following it, is the promise of Jehovah's return to Jerusalem with mercies, of the rebuilding of the temple, nay, of the whole area of the holy city, and of the spreading abroad of a new, unparalleled prosperity of its inhabitants; in short, of the "comforting of Zion" (1:16–17). All this plays within the limits of the holy land.

The second night-vision is that recorded in 1:18–21; the vision of the "horns" and of "the blacksmiths" (or "carpenters") sent to destroy them. These "horns" call to mind the role played by the horns in the night visions of Daniel. Still, this need not imply any direct or exclusive provenience of the symbolism from that quarter, for "horns" also occur in several other connections. According to Habakkuk 3:4, Jehovah himself has horns in his hands where they are the secret place of his strength. Closely related to this are the horns on the altar (Ex. 27:2). The wicked and the righteous both have horns (Ps. 75:10). The advent signifies the raising up of "a horn of salvation for Israel" (Luke 1:69). It will be observed that in most of these instances, the horns are conceived as attachments to some member or object. In Daniel especially, they appear as growing upon the heads of the world-kingdoms determining the sequence of their emergence and the degree of fierceness reached in the course of their development. The determination to be ruthless and unsparing in violent procedure is figuratively described as "taking horns" to one's self (Amos 6:13; 1 Kings 22:11). In the passage before us, they appear personalized. The pagan powers are, rather than have, horns. They stand for the powers that have scattered Judah, even Israel, and its center, Jerusalem. The latter name *Israel* does not stand here for the northern kingdom, but designates the territory of the southern realm in distinction from its capital.

The four *charashim* ("blacksmiths"), after a similar fashion, signify other powers come to fray the horns belaboring Israel and to break them. This again reminds us of the Danielic representation according to which each embodiment of the pagan world-power is removed out of the way by the next succeeding one.

When these deliverance-forces have completed their task, Jehovah is ready for the resumption of the people into his favor, which act is set forth in the third night vision symbolic of the act of restoration and the bestowal of new, unprecedented prosperity. This furnishes a (symbolic) duplicate to what was already held in prospect by the promise of 1:16–17. The symbolism adopted for this is that of the man with his measuring line (2:1). His plying of this line indicates that Jerusalem will again be inhabited as of old; yet so, as is significantly added, as is to become "a town without walls" (2:4). This particular feature is symbolical on the one hand of the safety from attack bestowed upon the future city and, on the other hand, of boundless multiplication of its inhabitants. The core of the new blessedness conferred after this fashion is described as the return of Jehovah himself; i.e., "the glory within." For this marks the innermost and uppermost treasure of Israel's relationship to Jehovah (2:5). The remainder of the chapter is descriptive of the judgment to befall the Gentiles to bring about the state of redemptive felicity promised to Israel. More particularly, there is joined to this new indwelling of Jehovah in the midst of his own people the promise that "many nations shall be joined to Jehovah in that day" (2:11); i.e., the promise of universalism of the true religion. The circumstances that this is predicated only of many, not of all nations, is hardly intended to serve as a restriction.

The fourth and fifth night visions are symbolic of a new, unprecedented significance and importance to be acquired by the high priestly office in the approaching period of restoration and of a new, intimate relationship to be established between the sacerdotal and the royal ministers of Jehovah's administration of the theocracy (chapters 3 and 4). The first factor in this consists of Joshua's absolute vindication from the charge of malfeasance in office laid against him by "the Adversary," a representation reminiscent of the prologue to Job. There is a difference, however, between the two situations as regards the pertinence of the charge made. In Job, the satanic suggestion is not one of actual default, but only of potential disloyalty. If God were to take away from Job the treasures of his prosperity, this would immediately reveal the self-interested character of his service of Jehovah, because it would cause him straightway to abandon the latter. Here, in the case of Joshua, the assumption is that some real ground for the unfavorable judgment passed does exist, because he is actually represented as one clothed in filthy garments (3:3). Nonetheless, Satan is rebuked for the very reason that his charge makes a personal deficiency and an irretrievable fault out of what seems to have been no more than the inevitable result of the precarious situation in which the priesthood had to labor during the captivity in the face of the desecration of its entire milieu and apparatus. Jehovah therefore rebukes the Slanderer with the reminder that Joshua resembles a firebrand plucked from the fire, which amounts to saying that since Jehovah had his positive purpose in regard to the future service of the chief priest and had been eager to rescue him in spite of all the above-named shortcomings, it amounted to impugning the justice and wisdom of God when Satan hinted at his unfitness to serve. Whatever inadequacy Joshua's present or immediately past circumstances might suggest, the removal of these is symbolized by the instantaneous investment with clean garments among which the miter, specifically the distinguishing accoutrement of the high priest, receives particular mention. If this involves a promise of future purity and adequacy of administration, the guarantee for the fulfillment of this promise is symbolized by the gift to Joshua of the stone on which the seven eyes of God are invariably fixed in order to secure the attainment of the great ends of the priesthood (3:9). Probably this representation of the sacred stone constantly kept by Jehovah before his eyes likewise suggests that even while the ruin of the temple structure prevents, for the present, the ideal worship due to God, nevertheless some intermediate provision is to be made for the resumption and continuance of the interrupted ritual service. Compare what is said in 4:7 about Zerubbabel's bringing forth the headstone of the new sanctuary with shoutings of "grace, grace unto it." In order to emphasize the intimacy of the new priestly ministration

with Jehovah the assurance is added that Joshua and the minis-
trants under him will be given places "among those that stand
by," that is among those that attend upon the throne of God, even
the angels (4:7). Finally, the sacrifice brought upon the stone provided will have the unique efficacy of removing the iniquity of the
holy land "in one day" (cp. 3:9; the *ephapax* of Heb. 7:27).

While it might almost seem as though, by this whole representation, the importance and indispensableness of the work of
Zerubbabel, the Davidide, the servant in regal office, were more
or less obscured, this would not be in accordance with the
prophet's intent. True, the ethical substructure is of fundamental importance. Yet in the physical sphere also a great hindrance
exists to the realization of the ideal held in prospect. This is characterized as "the great mountain before Zerubbabel" (4:7),
which is to become a plain. And this, as is significantly added,
will be brought about by the omnipotence of the Spirit, not by
might, nor by power (4:6); i.e., the outcome will depend not on
the physical might or power of those who seek to frustrate Jehovah's purpose, but by triumphant casting down of all resistance
through the divine Spirit. The symbolism of the candlestick all
of gold, with its bowl upon the top whence proceed the seven
lamps each with seven pipes and as feeders of the oil the two
olive trees at the side, serves to express the pneumatic provenience of all the energy required for the fulfillment of the divine
promise; for the "golden oil" stands, as oil does elsewhere, for the
Spirit. Hence Joshua and Zerubbabel are called in 4:14 "the two
sons of oil that stand by the LORD of the whole earth." Here again
the importance of the contribution that true sacrifice will render
toward the attainment of the end contemplated is brought out by
the assurance that Jehovah himself will provide, by his own
hand, the engraving upon the stone previously described (3:9).
And how truly this all weaves around the messianic Person may
be estimated from the fact that at the center of the entire pericope stands the statement "for, behold, I will bring forth my Servant, the Branch" (3:8). It is on account of this subservient
cooperation also of the priestly service to the messianic regime

that Joshua and his fellows, that sit before him, are called men of a sign with reference to the introduction of "the Branch," a designation pointing back significantly to Isaiah 8:18: "Behold I and the children which Jehovah has given me are for signs and wonders in Israel." The sixth night vision is made up of the flying curse-roll and the ephah filled with wickedness personified as a woman (chapter 5). On top of this a talent of lead is placed, so bearing down on the woman underneath it as to render escape impossible. The ephah is taken up by two other women with wings lifting it between earth and heaven and depositing it in the land of Shinar which is, according to Genesis 10:10; 11:2, the beginning and center of Babylon, the seat of the world-power hostile to the kingdom of God. This is a most realistic piece of symbolism in regard to which not the provenience of the woman, nor her personal character ought to be inquired into, since she is here significant on account of what she does, not on account of what she is.

In chapter 6 the prophet relates his last night vision. From a formal point of view it resembles the first, that of the man among the myrtle trees and of the riders of horses of other colors sent to walk to and fro through the earth. The difference lies in the point that the riders of chapter 1 are a patrol commissioned to take notice and report back what they have found in their reconnaissance to be the de facto condition of the earth, whereas here they appear as superhuman executors of the divine purpose. The four "winds" or "spirits" carry the vengeance of Jehovah in the four wind-directions; i.e., universally in every direction. Northward to Babylon, Assyria, Persia, etc. (the black horses-chariot symbolizing the darkness of death being followed up in this direction by the one with white horses, inasmuch as the vengeance of Jehovah's action is crowned by victory); southward the "grisled," i.e., "flecky," "spotted" horses ride toward Egypt and Ethiopia. This leaves the direction of the "red horses" of verse 2 unexplained, and the attempts to supply the deficiency are of uncertain merit because the text is not certain. It is further declared that the dispatch of the chariots toward the north has had the result of "quieting Jehovah's Spirit" (6:8). The divine resolve of vengeance has received satisfaction. Finally, it will be observed that these several chariots with their variously colored horses issue from between two mountains described as "mountains of brass" (6:1). Inasmuch as the entire action is obviously conceived as issuing from Jerusalem, Jehovah's earthly habitation, the proposal to interpret the two mountains as the Mount of Olives, on the one hand, and the temple mountain, on the other, commends itself. The mountains are of brass because of their unmovableness. Compare 14:4, where the Mount of Olives is cleft in its midst, one half being removed toward the east, and the other toward the west so as to leave a large valley between.

With the close of 6:8, the visionary mode of transmission of the prophecy ceases. In the place of "he showed me" or "behold I saw," the ordinary formula, "the word of Jehovah came unto me" is employed and the discourse turns into narrative. At the same time, and perhaps partly in consequence of this, the next pericope contains the essence and core of the entire book; viz., the investment of the royal figure with the high priestly office (6:9ff.). This is somewhat obscured by the circumstance that at first not Zerubbabel, but Joshua seems to be the recipient of the act. Jehovah commands pointedly that the prophet shall take the silver and gold that the emissaries of the still-in-exile remaining portion of the people in Babylon have sent to Jerusalem (6:11). They are to have made it into a crown ("crowns"), take it to a certain man's house (the house of Josiah, the son of Zephaniah) on the very same day, and there proceed to put the crown upon the head of Joshua, apparently in the presence of the three men who have brought the silver and gold, or its equivalent, with them. The sequel, however, forbids this understanding of the matter outright; for the narrative proceeds: "and speak unto him"; i.e., unto Joshua, "behold the man whose name is 'the Branch' he, etc." (6:12). The action in its last resort terminates not upon Joshua, but upon Zerubbabel. Not that Joshua becomes king, but that Zerubbabel through him is enabled to officiate in a high priestly capacity, is the salient point in the situation. Hence he can be "a priest upon his throne" without infringing upon the prerogatives of the priesthood. Precisely because this is so, no envy, no duplicity results. "The counsel of peace" is between them both. That the "Branch" grows up "out of his place" is a reference to the Isaianic picture of the cutdown trunk bound to sprout anew from underneath. Finally, a principle of universalism finds expression in 6:15: "they that are far off shall come and build in the temple of Jehovah," unless the phrase "far off" should be understood of the dispersion. The correctness of the above interpretation as a whole is borne out in the New Testament by Psalm 110 and the teaching of the epistle to the Hebrews on the high priestly office of Christ.

10. Malachi. The eschatological peculiarity of the discourses of this prophet consists, first of all, in the preponderance of the negative emphasis on the indictment for sin compared with which the positive message of the good things to come appears proportionately condensed and restrained. But this negativeness of the indictment of sin is still more strikingly brought out by the observation that the sin charged to the people's account bears, on the whole, a ritual character, although the social-economic elements reminiscent of the older prophets is by no means wholly absent. It is not, humanly speaking, a mere accident when the parting admonition of Jehovah, immediately before the conclusion of the book, assumes the form "remember ye the law of Moses, my servant, which I commanded unto him for all Israel in Horeb, even statutes and judgments" (4:4). The significance of this feature will become apparent from a brief enumeration of the delinquencies specified. These are as follows:

1. The bringing of polluted bread upon the altar, the bringing of blind, lame, sick, torn animals to the sanctuary for sacrifice (1:7–8, 13).
2. The subjective motivation underlying the offering brought: it is made in the spirit of "not for naught"; i.e.,

not in the mental attitude of unselfishness which alone can render a sacrifice acceptable to Jehovah. An inevitable result of this, when the anticipated quid pro quo did not materialize, a sentiment of ritual weariness, a pragmatic indifference arose even in regard to the maintenance of ceremonial religion.

3. The specific charge against the priesthood of connivance with these ritual malpractices. These amount to violation of "the covenant of Levi" (2:8). The ideal of the priestly office, to be a messenger of Jehovah in the teaching of true knowledge in ceremonial matters, is lost sight of (2:1–3; 3:14).

4. The failure to bring the prescribed tithes to the sanctuary (3:10).

5. The marrying of the daughter of a strange god and the disloyalty involved in this to the monogamous claims in force among Israel. The query "Did he not make one?," although he had abundance of life-giving Spirit at his disposal, refers to the creation of a single wife to be the helpmate of Adam (2:15).

The outstanding positively eschatological elements as, in part, determined by this negative substructure, are the following:

1. The promise of universalism—Jehovah's name will be great among the Gentiles. The chief embodiment of this will be that "a pure offering" will be brought from them to Jehovah in the widest compass—from the rising unto the setting of the sun, his name being great among the nations (1:11).

2. The coming of Jehovah to his temple—this means more than what was expected from the completion of the temple building, although it does not specifically hold in prospect the return of the Shekinah to the sanctuary (3:1; cp. Hag. 1:8; 2:3–9).

3. The judgment aspect of Jehovah's advent—the coming is condensed into the one "day" par excellence and this one day assumes the character of a veritable *dies irae* ("day of wrath") (3:2; 4:1).

4. Side by side with this retributory aspect, the judgment assumes the form of a process of purification resembling the method whereby pure silver and gold are extracted from the dross adhering to them. This is the old Isaianic conception (3:3).

5. The rising of the "Sun of *Zedaqah*" (4:2)—the latter term not to be confined to the the idea of guiltlessness through the removal of sin, although this is, of course, included. The very important positive elements of the concept ought not to be overlooked. These are "prosperity," "felicity," "salvation." It is difficult to render the pregnant term by one single equivalent. On the whole, Moffatt's "the saving Sun" at least approximates the richness of the manifold associations (cp. Jer. 23:6, *Jehovah Zidqenu*, where a similar limitation to the judicial aspect of the relationship [and that negatively considered] is equally unwarranted).

6. The idea of "the Rising Sun," in itself a common feature of the prophetic light-eschatology, may possibly here refer back, as it certainly does with Jeremiah and Zechariah, to the up-shooting of the messianic "Branch" in Isaiah. The term *anatole*, a common term to both the light and the botanical representations of the messianic epiphany, renders this a possibility to be reckoned with. For the fuller data on this point, compare the discussion of the term *Branch* in the chapters on Jeremiah and Zechariah.

7. A twofold mission is said to precede the "coming" of Jehovah. On the one hand, we have: "behold, I send my messenger [*maleach*] before me" (3:1). It is certainly a remarkable coincidence that the designation of the first precursor of Jehovah's coming *mal'akhi* is identical with

the name of the author of the prophecy, *malechi*. It has been, perhaps rashly, inferred from this that the name appearing in the title is a symbolic name, not the actual name of the writer. Reversely, one might conjecture that the introduction of the phrase *my messenger* was an adjustment of the idea intended to refer (in the actual case) to the name of the prophet. On the other hand, "behold, I will send you Elijah the prophet, before the great and terrible day of Jehovah comes" (4:5). For the New Testament application of this prediction to John the Baptist, cp. Matthew 11:11–15; Mark 9:11–13; Luke 7:19–30; John 1:21. The phrasing of the prophecy in the Malachi text does not necessitate the inference of an actual reincarnation of Elijah in the Baptist, but it permits of this construction which was, without doubt, the accepted exegesis of the passage in certain Jewish circles.

8. The specific task of Elijah is defined as a "turning of the heart of the fathers to the children, and the heart of the children to their fathers" (4:6). At first reading, this seems to presuppose a spiritual separation within the ranks of Israel in which, however, the departure from the theocratic correctness was evenly divided as between the elder and the younger elements. If this exegesis is adopted, both the elder and younger divisions are contemporaneous to the time in which the . . . [?] . . . activity of the Elijah redivivus belong; that is, speaking in terms of the New Testament fulfillment, to the time of the ministry of John the Baptist. It remains possible however that by the "fathers" are meant the pious ancestors of the later apostate Jews in the ancient periods of Israel's history. These fathers would, in that case, be represented as having retained in their postmortem state a lively interest in the experiences and destinies of their descendants during the later ages of history. In a general way, 1 Peter 1:10–12 might be compared with

the last mentioned exegesis, although Peter does not speak of the preoccupation of the Old Testament consciousness with the later period in general, but of the fore-searchings of the prophetic mind specifically.

NOTES

Chapter 1. Introduction

1 Of the above phrases, two already occur in the LXX as translations of the Hebrew phrase *acherith hajjamim: eschatai hemerai* (Gen. 49:1; Isa. 2:2; Jer. 37:24 [30:24]; Ezek. 38:16; Hos. 3:5; Mic. 4:1; Dan. 10:14); *eschaton ton hemeron* (Num. 24:14; Deut. 4:30; 31:29; Jer. 23:20; 25:18 [49:39]).

2 The Jerome quote is from the Vulgate of Job 19:25–27.

3 Augustine cites *et in carne mea videbo Deum* (Job 19:26) in *City of God* 22.29.4 (FC 24:501–2; PL 41:799).

4 For the Luther translation, cf. *Die Bibel oder die ganze Heilige Schrift das Alten und Neuen testaments. Nach der deutschen Unersetzung Martin Luthers* (Wurttembergische Bibelanstalt Stuttgart, 1970), 588 (note) on Job 19:25–27.

5 "One long night must be spent in sleep by us all," *Poems of Catullus* 5.6 (Loeb 6–7). (Ed.—I think this is what Vos is citing, although his text is different. Catullus reads, "Nobis, cum semel occidit brevis lux, nox est perpetua una dormienda.")

6 Virgil, *Aeneid* 6.679ff. (Loeb 1:552ff.).

7 Seems to be an allusion to *The Odyssey* 11.488–91(Loeb 1:420–21). I owe this suggestion to my daughter, Kristin Annette Dennison.

8 John Calvin, "Psychopannychia: Or a refutation of the error entertained by some unskilful persons who ignorantly imagine that in the interval between death and the judgment the soul sleeps, together with an explanation of the condition and life of the soul after this present life." In *Tracts and Treatises in Defense of the Reformed Faith*, trans. Henry Beveridge (Grand Rapids: Eerdmans, 1958), 3:413–90. For a recent evaluation of the work, cf. Willem Balke, *Calvin and the Anabaptist Radicals* (Grand Rapids: Eerdmans, 1981), 25–34; Timothy George, "Calvin's Psychopannychia; Another Look," in E. J. Furcha,

In *Honour of John Calvin, 1509–64* (Montreal: McGill University, 1987), 297–329.

9 Paul de Lagarde, *Ubersicht uber die im Aramaischen, Arabischen und Hebraischen ubliche Bildung der Nomina* (Osnabruck: Otto Zeller Verlag, 1972), 94.

10 Julius Wellhausen, *The Book of Psalms* (New York: Dodd, Mead, & Co., 1898), 164 (on Ps. 2), 176 (on Ps. 28).

11 Bernhard Stade, *Geschichte das Volkes Israel* (Berlin: G. Grote'sche Verlagsbuchhandlung, 1887), 1:413.

12 Julius Wellhausen, *Prolegomena to the History of Israel* (Edinburgh: Adam & Charles Black, 1885), 152–53.

13 Cf. Gustaf Dalman, *The Words of Jesus* (reprint; Minneapolis: Klock & Klock, 1981), 291. Cp. *Die Worte Jesu* (Leipzig: J. C. Hinrichs sche Buchhandlung, 1930), 238–39; also his *Studien zur biblischen Theologie: der Gottesname Adonaj und seine Geschichte* (Berlin: H. Renther, 1889), 82–83.

Chapter 2. Pagan Eschatologies

1 Vladimir S. Golenishcher/Golenischeff (1856–?) published Papyrus Leningrad 1116B in 1913: Les papyrus hieratiques nos. 1115, 1116A, et 1116B de l' Ermitage Imperial a St. Petersbourg. For an English translation, see *ANET* 1:144–46. Current dates for Pharaoh Snefru are ca. 2613–2494 B.C.

2 Cf. "The Admonitions of Ipu-Wer," *ANET* 1:441–44. The reference to the "shepherd" (i.e., herdsman) is on page 443. The document is currently dated 1350–1100 B.C.

3 This document is attributed to the reign of Egyptian King Bocchoris (ca. 718–12 B.C.). But the demotic text on a papyrus roll dates from the reign of Augustus Caesar (A.D. 7–8). The text of the prophecy is found in C. C. McCown, "Hebrew and Egyptian Apocalyptic Literature," *Harvard Theological Review* 18 (1925): 393–94.

4 The "Prophecy of the Potter" is Oxyrhynchus Papyrus 2332 ("The Oracles of the Potter"). It is a third-century A.D. Greek text (ca. A.D. 284)—cf. Oxyrhynchus Papyri (Oxford Microform Edition, 1981), 22:89–99. The English text is in McCown, "Hebrew and Egyptian Apocalyptic Literature," 398. It is attributed to Amenophis IV = Akhenaton (1379–1362 B.C.).

5 Hans Ostenfelt Lange (1863–1943).

6 The Leiden Papyrus.

7 Alan Henderson Gardiner.

8 Cf. A. H. Gardiner, *The Admonitions of an Egyptian Sage from a Hieratic Papyrus in Leiden* (Hildesheim: Georg Olms Verlag, 1909/1969), 13–14.

9 Ibid., 13–14, 78–80.

10 Gudea of Lagash.

11 The text is found in Henri Frankfort, *Kingship and the Gods* (Chicago: University of Chicago Press, 1978), 238.

12 Sargon I (ca. 2350 B.C.). Cf. inscriptions from Nippur and Kish in George A. Barton, *The Royal Inscriptions of Sumer and Akkad* (New Haven: Yale University Press, 1929), 343, 353.

13 Naram-Sin (ca. 2200 B.C.). For the text, see Frankfort, *Kingship and the Gods*, 224.

14 Ashurbanipal I (ca. 669–627 B.C.). See Daniel D. Luckenbill, *Ancient Records of Assyria and Babylon* (London: Historics and Mysteries, 1989), 2:291.

15 Berosus (ca. 330–250 B.C.) is cited by Seneca, *Natural Questions* 3.29.1 (Loeb 7:287).

16 For the 432,000 years, cf. *ERE* 2:533.

17 For Darmasteter's views on the age of Avesta, cf. *ERE* 2:270.

18 Wilhelm Bousset, *Die Religion des Judentums* (Tubingen: J. C. B. Mohr, 1926), 481ff.

19 "Eclogue IV" (Loeb 1:29–33).

20 Cf. "The Sibylline Oracles" 1.1–4 in James H. Charlesworth, ed., *The Old Testament Pseudepigrapha* (Garden City, N.Y.: Doubleday, 1983), 1:335.

21 Virgil, *Aeneid* 6.791ff. (Loeb 1:560–63).

Chapter 3. The Present Juncture in the History of Old Testament Eschatology

1 *Die vorexilische Jahveprophetie und der Messias* (1897).

2 *Schopfung und Chaos in Urzeit und Endzeit* (1895).

3 On this charge, see Werner Klatt, *Hermann Gunkel. Zu seiner Theologie der Religion- geschichte und zur Entstehung der formgeschichtlichen Methode* (Gottingen: Vandenhoeck & Ruprecht, 1969), 70.

4 *Der Ursprung der israelitisch-judischen Eschatologie* (1905).

Chapter 8. The Shiloh Prophecy

1 See *Christology of the Old Testament* (Grand Rapids: Kregel, 1956), 1:57–98, esp. 80ff.

2 August Dillmann, *Genesis Critically and Exegetically Expounded* (Edinburgh: T. & T. Clark, 1897), 2:462–65.

3 Franz Delitzsch, *A New Commentary on Genesis* (Edinburgh: T. & T. Clark, n.d.), 2:375–85.

4 Hermann Gunkel, *Genesis ubersetzt und erklart* (Gottingen: Vanderhoek & Ruprecht, 1977), 481–82.

5 Hugo Gressmann, *Der Messias* (Gottingen: Vandenhoeck & Rupreckt, 1929), 221–23.
6 Cf. Delitzsch, *New Commentary on Genesis*, 2:380–86.
7 Thus, the Samaritan text (cf. Brian Walton, *Biblia sacra polyglotta* [1657] 1:221), Targum Onkelos (cf. Moses Aberbach, *Targum Onkelos to Genesis* [KTAV, 1982] 284–86), the Peshitta (Syriac) (cf. Walton, 1:220), and LXX versions; also many church fathers, among whom is Justin Martyr.
8 Justin Martyr, *Dialogue with Trypho*, 120 (FC, 6:334).
9 Hengstenberg, *Christology of the Old Testament*, 1:93ff.
10 Ibid., 69.
11 Delitzsch, *New Commentary on Genesis*, 2:380.
12 Eusebius, *The Proof of the Gospel*, trans. W. J. Ferrar (New York: Macmillan, 1920), 1:21, 2:70.
13 Raymundi Martini, *Pugio Fidei adversus Mauros et Judaeos* (1687/1967), 316–17.
14 Pietro Galatino, *De arcanis catholicae veritatis*, 4.4 (1603), 197.
15 Delitzsch, *New Commentary on Genesis*, 379.
16 Cf. John Henry Kurtz, *Manual of Sacred History* (Philadelphia: Nelson S. Quiney, 1881), 72, 96.
17 Hengstenberg, *Christology of the Old Testament*, 1:79.

Chapter 10. The Balaam Oracles

1 Cf. Gregory the Great, "Praefatio," 6.13, Moralium libri, sive expositio in librum Job (PL 75:524).

Appendix: Additional Passages from Vos

1 Bernhard Duhm, *Die Psalmen* (Freiburg: J. C. B. Mohr, 1899), 214.
2 J. J. P. Valeton, *De Psalmen* (Nijmegen: H. Ten Hoet, 1913), 2:71, 74–75.
3 Friedrich Baethgen, *Die Psalmen: ubersetzt und erklart* (Gottingen: Vandenhoek & Ruprecht, 1895), 259.
4 W. Staerk, *Lyrik (Psalmen, Hohesleid und Verwandtes)* (Gottingen: Vandenhoek & Ruprecht, 1920), 145, 147–50.
5 Julius Wellhausen, *The Book of Psalms* (New York: Dodd, Mead, & Co., 1898), 199.
6 E. W. Hengstenberg, *Commentary on the Psalms* (Edinburgh: T. & T. Clark, 1857), 3:60–61.
7 Ferdinand Hitzig, *Die Psalmen* (Leipzig: C. F. Winter'sche, 1865), 2:204.
8 Symmachus (cf. PG 16:1045).
9 Aquila (cf. PG 16:1044).

10 For the Targum and Syriac, cf. Walton, *Biblia sacra polyglotta* (1657), 3:220–21.

11 Cf. Justus Olshausen, *Die Psalmen* (Leipzig: S. Hirzel, 1853), 347 on Ps. 84.

12 C. von Orelli, *The Twelve Minor Prophets* (Minnepolis: Klock & Klock, 1977), 304–11.

13 Stade, "Deuterozacharja: Eine Kritische Studie" ZAW 1 (1881): 1–96; 2 (1882): 151–72, 275–309.

INDEX OF SCRIPTURE